How to Canoe

almost get killed by rapi
bears, have your blood suc
mosquitoes, and ot

A True Story

by Jeff Farr

Old Barn Publishing
WWW.OBEPUB.COM
Old Barn Enterprises, Inc.
Carthage, NC

How to Canoe in Canada almost get killed by rapids, eaten by polar bears, have your blood sucked out by clouds of mosquitoes, and other fun stuff!

First print edition ISBN: 978-1-879009-39-4

To contact the author or publisher, visit obepub.com.

Disclaimer

Although the author and publisher have made every effort to ensure the completeness and accuracy of this book, we assume no responsibility for omissions, inaccuracies, or inconsistencies that may appear. To the extent that this book provides recommendations or comparisons, they represent only the opinions of the author.

Please note that this book describes the experiences of two people for the entertainment of the reader only. **It is not intended to be a guidebook.** It should therefor not be relied on for planning purposes. Maps and other descriptive information in this book may not depict current conditions. Anyone with an interest in taking a similar trip to the one described in this book should do their own due diligence and independent research and planning. Failure to do so may result getting killed by rapids, eaten by polar bears, your blood sucked out by clouds of mosquitoes, and other not-so-fun stuff.

This book is sold with the understanding that neither the author nor the publisher are engaged in rendering professional advice, or really, any advice at all. If expert assistance is required, the reader should consult with a competent professional.

The author and the publisher, therefor, shall have neither liability nor responsibility to any person or entity with respect to any loss or damage caused, or alleged to be caused, directly or indirectly, by the information in this book.

How to Canoe in Canada

almost get killed by rapids, eaten by polar bears, have your blood sucked out by clouds of mosquitoes, and other fun stuff!

A True Story

by Jeff Farr

Introduction

A special thanks to my friend and canoeing partner Fred Waters for giving me the "OK" to release this book to the general public. As you will see, there are some aspects to this story that some people may not want to have revealed.

And I did consider making some accommodating "edits."

But, in the end, I have left the manuscript essentially as it was written shortly after returning from our trip in 1982 — *for the historical record* — and because it captures the true spirit of the journey.

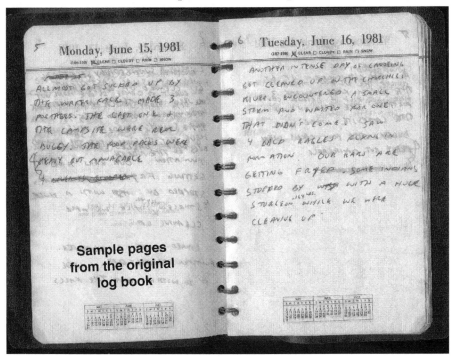

Sample pages from the original log book

If you're a photographer, you may be interested in the camera used on this trip. We needed something small and light, so the "Rollie 35" got the job. This is a <u>very</u> basic film-based camera with a fixed wide angle lens.

Most of the time the camera was packed away for its own protection,

5

and we were too busy trying to stay alive to worry about taking pictures, but the times it did see action, it did a pretty good job.

Now, to the Übercanoers and kayakers who may read this book and say, *"oh yeah, I could have done that backwards with one paddle tied behind my back."*

Maybe so... in your high-tech boat and these more modern times with better information, support services, and equipment.

On this trip, however, we had neither training nor technology on our side, and good information (like accurate maps and route descriptions), was hard to come by. Support services like drop offs, pick ups, equipment rentals, and accommodations, were also limited.

And do keep in mind that <u>real men don't use spray covers</u>.

So there. *Let's get started!*...

The following is a true story.

Even the names have not been changed to protect the stupid.

Origins

It was the summer of 1980.

I stood on the shore of a lake in northern Saskatchewan looking north.

Behind me was the northernmost road in the Province, and attached to it were all the other roads leading South to Tierra del Fuego.

Before me was The Wilderness... all the way to the north pole.

I wanted to see what was out there.

Fred Waters has been a friend since the 3rd grade and a partner on many insane adventures.

At this point in time, we had one primary thing in common — we were tired of working and bored with the Chicago area due to its lack of mountains, canyons, and wild beasts.

We decided that the remedy would be to quit our jobs, take the next summer off, hang out somewhere, and then relocate out west.

Since we both enjoyed canoeing, I suggested that we take a major trip in The Great Canadian Wilderness which would give us lots of time to read, write, play guitar, and relax.

And since we would have free lodging and could eat squirrels, it would also be cheap!

Being prone to blowing things out of proportion, our plans progressed from a four week trip down a river in central Ontario which was proven to be a good route for canoeing, to an 8 week expedition down a river in the Northwest Territories that had no record of being previously traveled.

In the end, our sense of self-preservation and our sense of adventure combined at mid-ground and we choose a route through the "Land of Little Sticks" that the Canadian Government advertised as canoeable, but for "Adventurous Experts Only."

Although we weren't sure if we qualified as "experts" — *having been on only two canoe trips before* — we knew we were <u>adventurous</u> and 50% isn't too bad for activities like this.

The biggest risk of the journey would be having only two people and one boat. If someone gets hurt — *or the canoe gets destroyed* — you're lunch meat for the bugs & bears.

However, finding <u>four</u> people who want to quit their jobs and live in the woods for eight weeks is difficult, even if you <u>are</u> going to the wonderful Land Of Little Sticks!

The route we chose had several advantages.

For one, it would take us through a variety of terrain — large lakes, small lakes, big rivers, little rivers, medium lakes, medium rivers, and rivers connected to other rivers that are connected to lakes of various sizes.

Also, as we went north, the trees would keep getting smaller and less numerous until we were in the treeless tundra. Which is why it's called the Land of "Little Sticks."

Another advantage of the route was the easy transportation connections. We would be able to take a train to our entry point just north of The Pas, Manitoba and we could hire someone to pick us up on Hudson Bay.

Plus, it was also possible to make arrangements to <u>rent</u> a canoe rather than drag our own all over North America.

We estimated our planned canoeing route would cover about 800 miles and take 8 weeks to complete. *The basic plan was...*

1. Drive from the Chicago area to The Pas, Manitoba, Canada.
2. Take a train about 120 miles north of The Pas to our starting point.
3. Canoe about 800 miles through lakes and rivers eventually ending at the mouth of the Caribou River on Hudson Bay.
4. Arrange for someone to pick us up on Hudson Bay and bring us to Churchill, Manitoba.

5. Take a train back to The Pas.

6. Head west to who knows where (we did not plan on returning to anywhere in particular).

Gathering all the information and equipment needed for the trip was a formidable task.

Over 100 letters were sent to various Canadian Government Agencies and that produced a stack of maps and pamphlets about two feet high.

Some of the information that was sent turned out to be very inaccurate because — *as we later learned* — despite what looked like detailed information on the area (like the locations of deadly rapids!), they were actually meant to be "artistic" posters and not really guide maps.

More on that later in this story.

Deciding what to take and where to get it proved to be a very time consuming task.

Little things, like how much toilet paper to take, become important on a trip of this duration. After a series of experiments, I was able to accurately calculate the number of shits-per-roll so we could figure out the exact amount of TP needed.

Another major challenge of preparation was to plan our wilderness cuisine.

At first we had discussed "living off the land," but we would have spent a lot of time finding and killing small creatures and then roasting them. A menu that was lightweight and nutritious needed to be found.

Freeze dried food was out because it's expensive, generally requires cooking, and doesn't taste good either (at least it didn't back then!).

Cooking definitely needed to be kept at a minimum because we didn't want to carry a lot of white gas for the stove, and building fires is tough when there aren't any trees!

Breakfast was no problem. In past trips, we had successfully used a combination of Roman Meal cereal and oatmeal mixed with non-fat dry milk and raisins. Each serving was sealed separately in a Seal-A-Meal bag and preparation merely required boiling some water and dumping it in.

Lunch was granola because it's high in calories, complete in nutrition and didn't require cooking. Plus, it could be eaten throughout the day. This was also sealed in individual servings.

Dinner was the problem.

After not enough research (as you will see later in story), natural brown rice was chosen for its quality of being very high in calories for its weight (we were trying to provide at least 5,000 calories per day).

The only problem with the rice was that it took so long to cook. So, I figured that if cereal companies can *puff* rice, we could pre-cook our rice by toasting it in the oven — mmm, crunchy.

Finding the right equipment was also a sizable task requiring numerous expeditions to various camping stores, as well as mail ordering stuff we couldn't find in Chicago (this was way pre-Internet).

The camping store people, of course, were all amazed that we were taking a trip of this magnitude with only two people and one canoe (*"if you crash or get hurt, you'll be dead!"* and *"you'll hate each other by the end of the trip"*).

We were amused by their concern.

Official List of Expedition Stuff

Food

65 lbs. Natural Brown Rice
75 lbs. Granola
30 lbs. Raisins
25 lbs. Nonfat Dry Milk
50 lbs. Cereal

2 months supply of Mega Vitamins
Total weight of food: 235 lbs.

Everything Else

2 Carlise Canoe Paddles
2 Stern Life Vests
A lot of Rope
1 Tent with Stakes
2 Sleeping Bags
2 Mosquito Head Nets
4 bottles of Insect Repellent
Repair Kit — tape, glue, nylon fabric, sewing stuff, safety pins, etc.
1 First Aid Kit
1 Signal Kit — mirrors, flares, and smoke bomb
2 ounces of Marijuana*
1 Pipe
4 packs of Rolling Papers
Lighters
2 Fishing Poles and Assorted Fishing Stuff
1 Fish Net
2 Guitars with extra Strings and Pegs
4 Water Bottles
Rain Gear
Biodegradable Soap
2 sets of Topographical Maps
Books
2 Backpacks with Personal Stuff (clothes, toothbrush, etc.)
1 Camera with Film

Total cost of food and equipment (1981 dollars) = $1,500.

> *Special note about the marijuana. First of all, those were different times. Second it was for medical purposes — you sure don't want to develop glaucoma when you have a lot of rapids to run! Lastly, for the record, we don't do that anymore.*

In addition to accumulating all the right stuff, we were getting in shape for the trip by running ten miles a day, swimming 3 miles a week, and lifting weights every other day.

In our spare time, we were taking accounting and marketing classes (essential knowledge for canoeing!) and trying to write a book (to drum up some cash).

This went on for about 6 months.

The Road North

The semester ended. We dropped the book idea. Our bodies were achieving the Greek Ideal. All items of equipment were collected. Our jobs were history.

On June 3, 1981, we threw everything in the back of Fred's pickup truck and <u>left town</u>...

Fred's Pickup Truck and some of our Stuff

Fred driving his pickup truck on the way out of town

We didn't get very far that first day. Two hours after leaving, we stopped at a friend's house for all the Mums champagne we could drink (and we can drink a lot!) and sampled a lot of vegetables (he was an investor in a vegetable company and had quite a few free samples for testing).

The next morning — *after breakfast and routine anti-hangover procedures* — it was non-stop to St. Paul Minnesota where we engaged in the sleazy motel routine and got a very bad smelling room...

"Excuse me sir, but the room you gave us has a very strong vomit-producing odor. You may want to check for dead bodies."

"Oh, really? I'll have to check on that, why don't you try this room?"

The second room wasn't as bad.

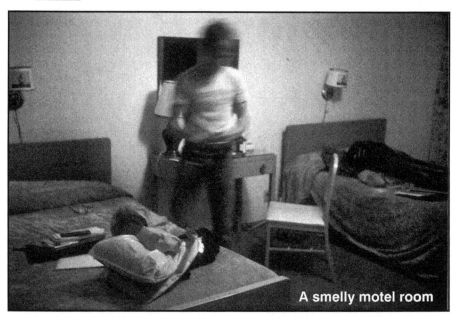

A smelly motel room

While in St. Paul, we frantically shopped for a few items we still needed but didn't have... you're never as ready as you think you are.

The next day we had a serious task to perform — get rid of all the drugs that were not hidden before we hit the Canadian border.

A valiant effort was made, but it was a task that eventually proved overwhelming.

Somewhere in Minnesota, about 25 miles from the Canadian border, there is a very happy garbage man.

Heading North To The Canadian Border

No one ever searches us anymore — we sailed right through the border and on to Winnipeg where we stopped at a camping store called The Happy Outdoorsman.

In a stroke of good luck, we met the owner, Harry Stimson, who had been to the area we would be canoeing in and he had written an article on it.

He invited us to his house for coffee, ice tea, and stories about the Wild North we would be visiting.

Harry gave us many good suggestions, including preventing us from canoeing down a river with no water. He found out about the "problem" the hard way and had to signal a plane to get flown out.

It was from Harry we that started getting an indication of what we were up against. His vivid descriptions of the bugs were downright scary. He also told us about his friend who was killed on the Seal River — a river near where we were going.

Harry also contradicted the Manitoba Government's assertion that we didn't need a <u>gun</u> while camping with the Polar Bears on Hudson Bay.

Special note — This is something we had specifically asked the Manitoba Government about and at the time we were happy to get their response that guns were not needed on Hudson Bay for Polar Bear safety. The problem is, Canada doesn't allow their regular citizens and tourists to legally have hand guns. So you can't just throw a .357 or .44 revolver in your pack. You have to bring a big, heavy, rifle or shot gun.

We appreciated all the advice and hospitality we received from Harry. The slogan on the Province's license plates says "Friendly Manitoba" and the residents seem to go out of their way to prove it. As good evidence of that, Harry sent us along with valuable information as well as some of his personal maps.

We made it to The Pas on June 7, 1981 in the midst of a blinding downpour.

We were now 1,400 miles — *mostly North* — from Chicago, but it really didn't seem that far.

Traveling north, the terrain change is minimal — just endless pine forest, although the trees near The Pas <u>are</u> a bit scrawny.

The town itself looks like a small Wisconsin town.

One considerable difference between The Pas and a small Wisconsin town, however, is the quantity of Drunken Indians. They are everywhere, falling over in the streets at all hours of the day. This, compounded with a communications problem and an obvious lack of prosperity, makes for a bad first impression of the area.

Another distinction between The Pas and its Southern counterparts is that it was barely over 50 degrees and everyone was wearing t-shirts and shorts. The weather tends to range on the cool side up there, so I guess the 50 degrees is a heat wave.

Our stay in The Pas was quite hectic. We hadn't settled down from our six months of getting ready — and we still weren't ready! A few items still needed to be purchased, such as a small pipe for the pot. After looking in almost every store in town, we found one in a combination sex and head shop.

Arrangements also needed to be made for the train ride to our drop off point where we would begin canoeing. A nice feature of the Canadian Rail Service in that area is they will conveniently drop you off anywhere in the woods you want.

Since we couldn't take the pickup truck with us on the canoe trip, we needed to find a place to store it while we were gone. And, of course, we had to pick up our <u>canoe</u>...

While we were still in the Chicago area, Fred had made arrangements with a fishing store owner to rent a 17-foot aluminum canoe. It sounded good on the phone, however, when we went to pick it up we had a BIG SURPRISE — it was a <u>square stern</u> canoe.

A square stern canoe is designed to travel large lakes with a motor — its flat bottom and large keel (a 1-inch deep "rudder" that ran the length of the boat) helps it track better under power. The flat bottom, however, increases friction, making it laborious to <u>paddle</u> in open water, and the large keel makes it unresponsive in rapids.

*Harry Stimson seemed to be very concerned that we wouldn't make it in anything but a Grumman expedition style canoe and mentioned it several times. We were also concerned — but — it was there, we were there, and there was no other choice within 200 miles. **It got the job.***

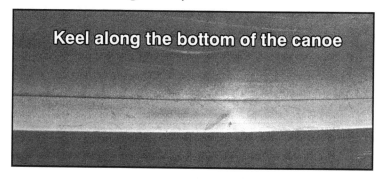
Keel along the bottom of the canoe

While in The Pas, we stayed at a campsite just outside the city and worked on packing and arranging our stuff for the trip.

We also worked the two bottles of whiskey that were given to us just before we left. Hard liquor, of course is an essential ingredient when making those last minute "life or death" pre-expedition decisions!

And there <u>were</u> some problems.

The most critical problem was that, while the food bags were able to <u>hold</u> all the food, they weighed 120lbs. each, and could not be carried very far (like on a 1.5 mile portage up hill!).

After a couple of "test portages" we redistributed some of the 235 pounds of food into the packs so that we could pick everything up.

We were now ready, done with hanging out at the camp site, and anxious to leave on our journey.

Our stuff with a bottle of Jack Daniels (on the stump, <u>no</u> we didn't take it with us... friends don't let friends canoe drunk!)

The Bizarre Beginning

It was Wednesday June 10, 1981, departure day.

The train from The Pas is scheduled to leave at 10:00am, but we are informed that it never really leaves until 11:45, which gave us time to search for a mosquito head net.

On the previous night, Fred had discovered that he left this essential piece of equipment in Chicago. We figured that being in the heart of mosquito and fishing country, finding a replacement would be no problem.

Such was not the case and Fred was the entertainment for the morning as he frantically ran from store to store in a last-minute effort to find one.

The item was finally found at the last possible place we could have looked.

Despite the shopping event, we still had time for breakfast and lively conversation...

"I can't believe we're finally leaving."

"It's going to take two weeks to settle down from getting ready."

"At least we can relax on the train now."

As we stepped onto the train we passed through a Time Warp and into the Twilight Zone. The train was about 50 years old, filled with Drunken Indians, and crawled along at about 20 miles an hour.

The Indians kept getting drunker as we went along.

They would come over, hang on us, and mumble things we could barely make out. One brought a female to us, grabbed her by the crotch and asked, *"You like fucky? You like fucky?"*

The only other white person on the train was a young man from Switzerland. He kept us entertained by telling us how we could waterproof our gym shoes with fish guts.

21

After <u>6 hours</u> and <u>120 miles</u> of this we were quite **glad** to get dumped off in the <u>middle of nowhere</u>.

It was now 5:00pm, and fortunately, since it stays light very late, we still had time to canoe.

The sun sets, but it never gets dark

The big problem now, was how to fit all our stuff in the canoe... something we weren't able to experiment with before we left The Pas.

At first glance, it didn't look possible. But after a half hour of experiments, we found a workable solution.

With everything successfully crammed into the canoe, we headed out onto the lake and immediately got disoriented. The profusion of islands, and not being familiar with the map scale, makes getting lost very easy!

After two hours of paddling, we were exhausted.

Having had an eventful and tiring first day, it was now time to find an ideal campsite and enjoy the <u>solitude of true wilderness</u>.

It didn't take long to find a good spot.

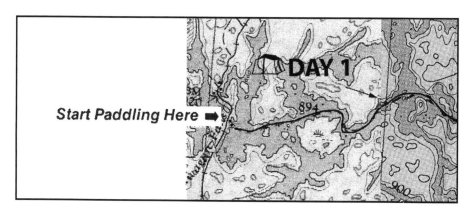

Start Paddling Here ➡

DAY 1

But as we pulled the canoe onto a beautiful sandy beach, we heard a soft buzzing sound.

In the distance we spotted a small motor boat headed our way.

It pulled up to our campsite and contained four Indians. They did not appear to be drunk.

We said *"Hi."*

They said *"Hi"* back and then proceeded to stare at us.

All our attempts at conversation seemed to fall flat. We began to feel a bit uncomfortable, especially since they had rifles and we didn't. Were we invading their territory? Camping on a Sacred Spot?

"That's quite a fish, what kind is it?," we remarked about the huge fish that was in the bow of the boat.

"Jackfish," they replied.

"Did you catch it with a line?"

"Yes."

They continued to stare at us. One asked, *"Do you want the fish?"*

We said that it was more than we could eat and thanked them for the offer.

They started their engine and left.

That was just plain weird.

We made camp, ate dinner, sat on a rock, and got stoned out of our minds. It had been a long day. But it wasn't over yet. Upon finishing getting stoned we heard another buzzing sound accompanied by a visual sighting of a boat headed our way.

This time, there were only two Indians in the boat and there was something very large underneath a tarp. The Indians were very proud as they pulled back the tarp. We were horrified — they had killed our childhood cartoon hero, Bullwinkle the Moose!!!

OK, everyone's gotta eat, and fortunately, these Indians were more communicative than our first visitors.

They explained that this was their first hunt and their father would be very proud when they returned with the moose. He would also be relieved since they were a day late!

We learned a little about the Indian culture from these Indians. For one thing, it is bad luck to leave a moose head at the kill site which is why they had the whole moose with them.

Meanwhile, two more boats pulled up with Indians and insulation for an ice house they were building. The moose hunters took off. Soon thereafter, the others also left. It was our first day in the wilderness and we had more visitors in one night than we would have had in a week back home!

Our first campsite

24

The First Days

The thought of being out in the wilderness for sixty days was a little overwhelming at first. No longer could we grab a beer and burger any time we wanted. For the next two months, it would be toasted rice, granola, oatmeal, and water.

In the wilderness, life gets down to basics. Things that are normally taken for granted and given little thought in "civilization" — *like where to eat, sleep, and being careful enough to not get injured* — become big decisions.

It doesn't take long, however, to adjust to the new surroundings. The senses tune into the environment, becoming much more sensitive without the deadening effect of noise and pollution found in the city. For example, you can tell when an animal is around and you can feel what the weather is going to do.

Fred

Jeff, author
of this book

Speaking of <u>weather</u>, Harry Stimson's prediction about the weather, unfortunately, seemed to be accurate — cool and damp. They had only 5 sunny days out of 30 on their trip. We were hoping we wouldn't have 50 wet and damp days out of 60 on ours!

Day 2

We put in a good day of paddling our first full day out.

Despite all the exercise done in preparation for the trip, the only way to <u>really</u> get in shape for canoeing all day is to canoe all day.

So we were pretty beat by the end of the day.

Being tired and having developed an appetite, we decided to try the legendary Fishing of The North.

Neither of us knew much about fishing. Before leaving, we bought two Eagle Claw pack rods which were the strongest compact gear we could find (we were warned that a large Northern Pike, a common fish in the area we were canoeing, could snap a weak rod!).

Next, we grabbed a bunch of lures — <u>something</u> was bound to work!

Our final attempt to prepare ourselves for fishing was buying a short book on the subject where we were warned that pike are the equivalent of fresh water sharks. Unchanged for millions of years, they survive by eating <u>anything</u> in their path. To prove the point, the book showed pictures of pike being caught with a cigar butt.

So, armed with the latest in fishing technology and information, we headed into the lake. Trying to think like fish, we found a small cove that looked like a good place for fish to hang out.

No luck.

We cast a few more times. No luck. I never did like fishing and began to get bored, so I stopped casting and began to play with my lure in the water by the edge of the boat.

"I don't think there are any fish in here, maybe we should try fishing somewhere else."

Just then a large pike hit my lure and nearly ripped the pole out of my hand, but I hung on.

During our fishing shopping we noticed that there were small bats for sale, and now it occurred to us why — pike are known to have sharp teeth, and as mentioned before, bite at anything. My grandfather once told me a story about a guy who had his arm bitten off by a barracuda, and we sure didn't want a repeat experience.

So after carefully netting the fish and bringing it into the boat, we found a new use for our canoe paddles — whack!

One dead pike and one bloody canoe paddle.

It wasn't long before Fred caught another pike which made <u>two</u> dead pikes and one <u>very</u> bloody canoe paddle with some fish guts stuck to it.

The Canadian lakes are great for fishing if you know what you're doing.

We didn't.

Even though I'm not much of a fishing enthusiast, I'll admit that hooking a fish and pulling it in is good fun — *especially if it puts up a good fight* — although the pike we caught just about jumped into the boat.

Cleaning a fish, however, more than makes up for any fun catching them.

Pike are especially hard to clean and we certainly didn't have the technique perfected. The two fairly large fish we caught didn't yield us much more than a few scraps of flesh. But as we cooked and ate our mangled meat, we were treated to a beautiful sunset, complete with a bald eagle flying in the horizon.

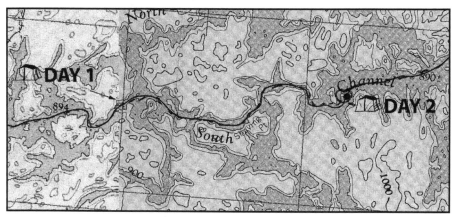

Day 3

The beautiful sunset and hopes of a sunny day were gone when we woke the following morning. It was cold, damp, and cloudy. We canoed for five hours and were exhausted, still not used to the strain of paddling a 700lb. canoe.

Aside from our arms being tired, our butts were taking a beating from sitting on the hard aluminum seats all day. As a result, our life preservers became seat cushions.

We had, however, made it to the base of Highrock Lake, the first of several huge lakes we would have to cross.

That night we had a conference about the rice.

I had spent a considerable amount of time toasting the 75 pounds of rice so that we could eat it without cooking. The problem was — *toasted or not* — the unboiled rice was not really edible. I had been trying to chew it, but couldn't get more than 1/3 of a bag down and Fred had been <u>swallowing it whole</u>.

We wondered if *that* did any good, or did it come <u>out</u> the same way it went <u>in</u>?

Fred with a bag of the questionable cuisine. He doesn't look real happy with me, does he?

And this brings us to another major event of the day.

Our first outdoor shit occurred today, and I mention this because many people unfamiliar with the outdoors have asked me, *"What do you do when you have to take a crap in the woods?"*

Since this seems to be such a major mystery, and not adequately covered in other camping literature, I will now attempt to address the issue and give you a preview of why proper technique is <u>important</u>...

First of all, the outdoors is actually one huge outhouse used fairly indiscriminately by <u>billions</u> of animals every day, so our contribution to the collection is minimal.

Regardless of this fact, to many humans, some locations for "taking care of business" are better than others. For example, the ecology minded will choose a spot away from water sheds, a shy person may roam deep into the woods, a sightseer may choose a place with a nice view, and a creative person will be, ~ *well* ~ creative!

The local topography and geology will also have a bearing on the <u>strategy</u> you use. In the area of Canada we were in, it is usually easy to find a <u>level</u> spot with <u>thick moss</u>.

So... the first step would be to cut a circle in the moss with a small shovel, pull out the moss in one big chunk, and set it aside.

The next phase is to "drop trow" and get into a squatting position.

This requires a bit of <u>balance</u> and some practice to get your <u>aim</u> down. The objective is to hit the hole and miss your shoes. Pulling the cheeks (not the ones on your face) apart with your hands can aid in avoiding long and messy wiping.

Wiping also takes some balance and can be tricky if your legs start getting tired.

The last steps are the reverse of the first — trow up, and moss back in the hole.

This entire procedure is known as "Squatting" or "Dropping Logs" and **it can be a <u>critical</u> skill when the bugs are bad and <u>speed</u> is a factor** — more on *that* later.

Rocky terrain can make certain "bathroom functions" difficult.

Fortunately we had ample amounts of "good ground" for everything we needed to do.

Day 4

The next day was sunny and about 75 degrees. We were too fatigued to canoe and decided to take the day off and hang out. Drinking coffee, playing guitars, reading, lying in the sun, smoking pot, it was the kind of day that make trips like this worthwhile and dispelled the theory that it would rain for two months!

A nice day is a great time to break out the dress whites.

Fred, of course, is just plaid to be alive.

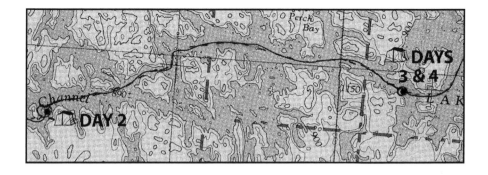

Day 5

Having rested a day, we were full of energy and our bodies were finally getting used to the canoeing.

The weather was perfect again. The scenery, of course, was magnificent. We were in prime Canadian Shield country.

The Canadian Shield, also known as the Laurentian Plateau, is a massive sheet of Precambrian rock extending over approximately half of Canada. In this area, the glaciers scraped off much of the topsoil exposing the rock. This makes for rugged shorelines of extreme beauty and provides many excellent camping sites (in areas where the shield is not exposed, the trees tend to come right to the shoreline making camping difficult and buggy).

The Canadian Shield,
~ aka ~ The Laurentian Plateau

The boreal, or pre-tundra forest, compliments the rocky shoreline quite nicely. The trees in the area, although smaller than in the South, are still quite abundant and add a wonderful pine smell to the crisp and clean Northern air.

The water in this area is crystal clear and safe to drink anywhere without treatment.

To add interest, each lake has its own flavor. I suppose the amount and variety of algae, minerals, and fish pee makes the difference. The best water is generally found at the end of a rapid because it has picked up minerals and has been aerated from rampaging over the rocks.

A <u>cold</u> drink can always be had by tying a rock to the water bottle and lowering it into the depths with a rope.

Naturally flavored water.

All the incredible scenery on such a pleasant day with no one around for miles and miles and miles required that we take frequent breaks and smoke a doobie.

To accomplish this, Fred would crawl to the back of the canoe and roll a joint on my pack.

A Doobius Area

Then we would smoke it.

Next, Fred would crawl back to the front of the canoe and tell stories.

"Ever here the one about...?"

I always said no, even if I heard it 10 times before. Besides, unless the wind was blowing my way, I couldn't really hear what he was saying anyway.

We put on quite a few miles that day and made it all the way to the top of Highrock Lake.

We had a sense of accomplishment making it across the first big lake.

The lakes <u>look</u> big on the map, but they seem even <u>bigger</u> when the only way to cross it is to paddle and paddle and paddle!

Because of our slower-than-expected progress, we were starting to become concerned that we might not make our pickup rendezvous on Hudson Bay.

That would be serious stuff, as you will learn a little later in this book.

But now — *on day 5* — we were camped on a beautiful island, and tomorrow, we would portage our first <u>waterfall</u> and enter the Churchill river system.

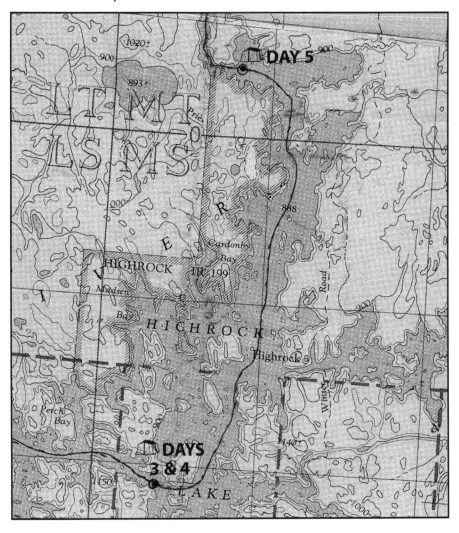

Day 6

It wasn't far from our Day 5 island campsite to the waterfall that leads out of Highrock Lake.

As we neared the top of the lake, the current picked up substantially. After all, there's an entire lake full of water wanting to get past a relatively small outlet. If you're a canoer, being part of the flow is something to be avoided.

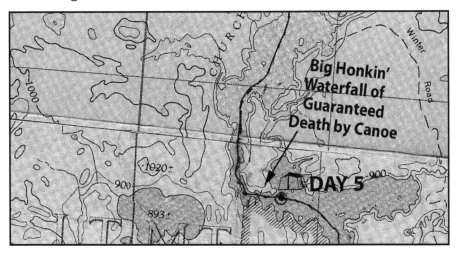

We knew from the map provided by the Manitoba Government that the waterfall could be portaged, so we headed to the side we thought the trail was on.

Securing the canoe from the current, we went to find the portage trail.

No trail was to be found — just a steep drop off. Portaging would be extremely difficult on this side if not impossible.

We did, however, get a good look at the falls which were aesthetically quite pleasing, but would definitely cause death to canoers.

Hoping to find the portage trail on the other side of the falls, we canoed against the current back towards the lake a bit, and then began paddling towards the other side of the waterfall.

Suddenly, about halfway across, we noticed that the current had grabbed us and we were moving <u>towards</u> the waterfall.

And rather quickly.

Sensing our precarious situation we yelled PADDLE!!! — *aimed our canoe <u>away</u> from the falls* — and paddled as hard as we could.

This produced a situation in which we were no longer getting closer to the falls, but **we weren't moving away from it either**.

At this point, my mind quickly assessed the situation...

Fact #1 — the waterfall is like a giant blender.

Fact #2 — if we get sucked in, we will be liquefied.

Fact #3 — we are paddling as hard as we can and <u>not</u> moving.

Fact #4 — we can't keep this up for very long.

PADDLE!!!... Somehow bodies have an extra reserve for times like these, and for only the second time in my life I felt the **Emergency Floodgates of Energy** open up, and I assume Fred's did, too.

Our collective power surge slowly — *but surely* — moved us to safety.

After putting our hearts back in our chest, we yelled at ourselves for being stupid and almost getting killed, and then laughed a lot.

A quick sketch made shortly after almost canoing over a waterfall.

Portaging around the waterfall involved making three trips.

First round included the 120 pound food packs, hiking boots, and paddles.

On the second trip, we took the frame packs, guitars, and day packs.

The canoe was always the worst, so we saved it for last.

We made 3 portages that day. The last was around Granville Falls where we avoided a repeat, almost-canoed-over-a-big-waterfall, performance.

Our campsite that night was the first one that was buggy, but it still wasn't too bad.

We were wondering where the legendary bugs of the north were.

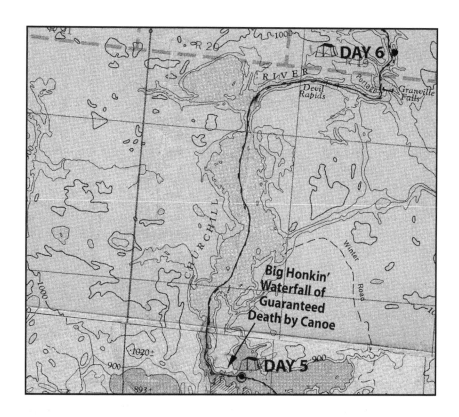

Day 7

Our strength was beginning to reach the point where we could canoe all day and not be too exhausted.

Wanting to make some distance, we embarked on an intense day of canoeing.

The day was one in which it looked like it was about to violently storm at any time, but never really did. At one point, we were caught in a light shower, and another time we waited for an impending storm while we got stoned under a tree, but none showed up.

In the afternoon the weather began to clear up and we decided it was time to clean the scum from our bodies.

The water in the Churchill river wasn't extremely cold, but it wasn't very warm either, so our immersion was brief.

We also washed our clothes, and while waiting for them to dry, we sat on a rock and got stoned. Of course, some Indians stopped by right after we were totally blasted.

These Indians had a really big fish — a 164-pound sturgeon they had netted by Granville Falls.

All clean, we continued our journey down the Churchill River to Granville Lake in nice sunny weather.

As we cruised down the river we spotted four huge birds flying in formation, one on top of the other, paralleling our motion. They turned abruptly, and as their heads hit the sunlight, four white dots glowed in the sky — bald eagles... always an inspiring sight!

The bright sun was also having a affect on us. Being in an aluminum canoe on the water tends to intensify the sun's rays, and even this far north, the rays were strong enough to begin to give us a good tan.

Unfortunately, our <u>ears</u> were taking a beating — so much that we were beginning to fear for permanent damage as the upper tips were getting crusty. We never thought we would need suntan lotion this close to the arctic!

That evening we camped on an island. It was a nice evening, but eventually the wind started to blow, the temperature dropped, and the humidity went up.

In short, it got <u>miserable</u>.

The morning brought no relief. We ate breakfast, packed our gear, pushed off into the cove and began paddling into the wind.

It didn't take us long to realize that we were slowly going <u>nowhere</u>.

Turning around — *with the wind at our backs* — it took us an easy 2 minutes to cover the same distance it took a hard 15 minutes to cover going in the other direction.

A new experience was about to become ours — being **windbound**!

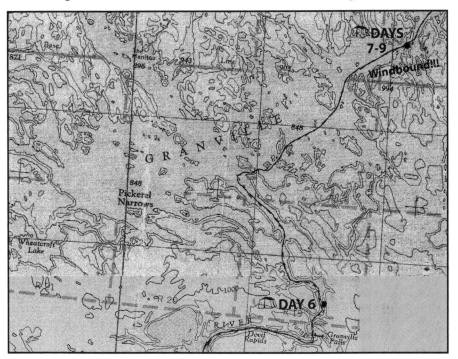

Day 8

We knew we'd be stuck for a while, so we gathered a bunch of rocks and wood for a campfire.

While arranging some rocks, I looked up just in time to see Fred, who was carrying a large boulder, slip on some algae and fall on his back with the boulder on top of him.

Figuring that he had broken his back or at least a few ribs, I started to think about how I would have to strap him on the canoe and go look for help.

But, Fred jumped up, *"I'm OK, I'm OK!"*

Things to do while windbound — drink coffee, get high, drink coffee, get high, play guitar, get high, play guitar, get high, drink coffee, write poems...

A Windbound Poem

It was a grey cold day,
when we sailed away,
the wind beneath our feet,
We left behind,
parts of our mind,
and an awful lot of meat.

And now we wonder if we shall be,
High under sunny skies,
Or tossed over a waterfall,
And severed from our thighs?

Will we return with memories,
that forever we can keep?
Or get pounded down into the ground,
in a bloody lifeless heap?

The first few days were rotten,
windy, damp, and cold.
Dry socks we had forgotten,
our feet were growing mold.
But then the sun it chose to shine,
And we dreamt of ice cold beers,
Our backs got tan, our faces red,
and we really fried our ears.

But then, from the arctic,
there came a roaring sound,
With wind so fierce
and waves so high,
It kept us on the ground.

So we sat before the fire,
And smoked up lots of weed,
And now I give these pages,
To Mr. Fred to read.

We also read books.

We brought several cheery ones with us. One was about the 14th century (plague time). Another was about Jim Morrison called, "No One Gets Out Of Here Alive," which I didn't like having with us because of the implications of the title on our current situation.

Our windbound campsite

The high point of our windbound day was a tour of the island, which didn't take very long since the island wasn't very big, but it's nice to know where you're stuck.

As evening set in, we stopped drinking coffee, ate dinner, and went to sleep dreaming of a full day of canoeing the next day.

Day 9

The following morning was exactly like the preceding and we were still grounded.

This was getting annoying. And it was also getting to be a <u>problem</u>.

What if we were stuck here a long time? Would this be a regular experience? We were already behind schedule. Missing our pickup on Hudson Bay would result in a lot of worried people, not to mention the logistical problem for us. In discussing the situation, we decided it was necessary to find an Indian with a motorboat to take us across the <u>immense</u> South Indian Lake.

The rest of the day was spent as the previous day.

Insanity began to set in.

Day 10

Friday June 19, 1981. The wind decreased in intensity. We packed our gear, and this time, made it out of the cove and into the main lake.

The entire day was a struggle. If the wind was any stronger, canoeing would not have been possible. Only determination and incredible strength — *our arms were starting to look like Popeye's!* — allowed us to make some distance.

South Indian Lake

It was about 30 miles to South Indian Lake, a long haul in a canoe.

Reaching the lake, we were greeted by a massive expanse of water, fanning out in all directions as far as the eye could see.

Also extending as far as one could see were <u>dead trees</u>. It seems that South Indian Lake — *and this was <u>news</u> to us* — is the site of a dam project that raised the water level about 10 feet. This significantly changed the topography and eliminated every practical camping spot. Where there was once a shoreline, there were only the tops of dead trees sticking above the water.

We were totally exhausted from the day's activities, but we didn't know what to do, so we just kept canoeing.

After an hour or two (or maybe three) we finally found a clearing with a cabin on it. Not knowing or caring whether the person owning it would mind if we camped there, we pulled onto shore, lacking any other place to go.

Finding the cabin unoccupied, we set up camp in a clearing nearby. Tired after a long day of work, we immediately got stoned. Of course, as soon as we were ripped, we heard the sound of a motor boat.

A young Indian pulled up.

Seeing the boat as an opportunity to get to the top of the 120 mile lake, we asked the Indian if he would take us for a fee. He said yes, and said he would be back in the morning.

Totally elated with our good fortune, we got really stoned.

As soon as we did, another boat pulled up (actually it was the same boat).

This time it had the boy's father. He explained to us how big the lake really was and that he could not even carry enough gas in his boat to get us to where we wanted to go. Instead, he offered to take us to Fish Camp #3. From there, we could catch the supply boat which goes to Loon Narrows, the northernmost settlement on the lake.

He wanted to leave right now.

Of course we accepted the offer and hastily broke camp.

When we left, it was about 10:00 pm.

> Since we were now about 57 degrees North and two days before the summer solstice, it remains fairly light all night long. So traveling by boat across the lake at night was perfectly practical. The brightness is about the same as when the sun just sets — perpetual twilight. The "Land of the Midnight Sun", where the sun does not sink below the horizon, was still to the North, being defined by the Arctic Circle which is at 66°30' North.

What a ride!!! The lake was as smooth as glass, the night air cool, and light formed incredible shadows and silhouettes in hues of deep blues and greens as we sped between the numerous islands.

And to add to the effect, we were stoned out of our minds!

Eventually, we arrived at beautiful Fish Camp #3.

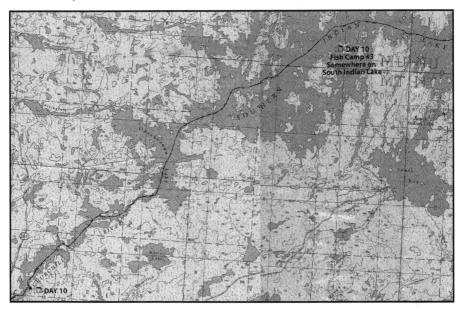

One would think that Indians living in such a pristine wilderness would be careful about the environment.

Such is not the case.

Indian camps we experienced were marred by numerous piles of garbage and Fish Camp #3 was no exception. It was difficult to find a place to camp. All the good spots were taken by garbage heaps. I know they don't have weekly garbage pickups, but at least they could have kept the trash in <u>one</u> spot.

Aside from garbage piles, the fish camp consisted of an ice house and a building with a well insulated room. Here the Indians would leave their fish covered with ice for the supply boat to pick up.

In return, the supply boat would leave gas for their boats.

Fish Camp #3

Day 11

The next morning we were up early to wait for the boat. Quite a few hours went by and no boat.

Some Indians showed up to pick up some ice and drop off fish. They assured us that there <u>was</u> such a thing as a supply boat, but they didn't know when it would come.

So we waited.

Finally we heard a motor. A fairly large boat appeared on the horizon and soon it pulled up to the dock. We asked them if we could get a lift and they said sure.

But first, we helped them fill 50 gallon drums with gas.

Since this was to be used in motor boats, oil had to be added. I cringed as the Indians poured oil in the gas and then threw the empty cans into the water leaving a nice oil slick in the otherwise clean and clear lake.

It was sunny and perfectly calm when we left Fish Camp #3. The lake, once again, was perfectly calm. We sat back, drank tea provided by the boat operators, and enjoyed the scenery, our spirits lifted greatly by our good luck.

It was a long ride to Loon Narrows. Again, it's a <u>big</u> lake.

When we arrived, the entire community seemed to come down to greet the boat. We helped unload the supplies and then took off in our canoe.

Heading straight North, the sun was warm, the air perfectly clean, and a gentle breeze was blowing.

Along the shore were some log cabins and canvas tents. The whole scene looked like a frontier community in the early 1800's. The sound of a harmonica in the distance completed the effect and it felt like we were on the edge of civilization which we sort of were.

It wasn't long, however, before the <u>1800</u>'s illusion was snapped. A motorboat approached us from the south, and came along side our canoe...

"Where are you going?"

"To the top of the lake."

"Do you want a ride?"

"Sure!!!"

It was a little tricky getting the canoe straddled on the small motorboat but we managed.

The young Indian explained that he could not take us <u>all</u> the way to the top of the lake, but he would take us as far as his camp. He was living with his family who lived in the wild during the summer. During the winter, the men trap while the kids go to school in the village which is at the south end of South Indian Lake.

After talking a while, our new Indian friend suggested that we spend the night with the family, and in the morning he <u>would</u> take us all the way to the top of the lake.

We accepted.

Our night with the Cree Indian family was a high point of the trip. I don't know if I have ever felt more at home.

The boy's father, John, was in his 60's and had a laugh that would put anyone at ease.

We talked until late at night about where we were going and where we came from. We made an attempt at explaining what it is like living in a place where there are 7 million people in the same space they have 200, but somehow I felt it was beyond their comprehension.

The boy who had picked us up said that he was going to visit the south — *meaning Michigan and Minnesota* — next summer. We gave him our contact information in case he, and we, made it back to Chicago at the same time.

John told us a bit about the land we were going to see in the next part of our journey although he had never been as far North as we planned on going. He thought we were <u>nuts</u>, especially when he heard that we were going to camp on Hudson Bay without a gun.

John <u>had</u> been far enough north to have stories about clouds of black flies that looked like pillars of smoke. We were starting to wonder about the flies. The supply boat guys said they had just brought back a couple of canoers that turned back because they couldn't take THE BUGS.

We also talked about South Indian Lake, how beautiful it used to be, and how the fishing turned sour after the dam was built.

Meanwhile, the younger members of the family had gotten ahold of our guitars and were jamming up a storm. John's wife fed us boiled fish and Banoc Bread (a bread that is made over a camp fire). It was delicious, especially considering the diet we had been on!

The Indians always keep a fire going with a pyramid made of branches over it. On the tripod was a grid with whitefish which would slowly smoke over the fire. It was here I began to feel I was in the far North. It was now June 21 and we were informed that there was still ice on the lake 3 days ago.

John (standing) with his family

Fred (center right), and whitefish cooking

Day 12

The next morning we were taken to the north end of South Indian Lake. We bid our Cree friends farewell and prepared for the rest of our journey, our spirits high.

Little did we know what was in store for us now.

A Moose Skull in the sand...

...would we soon be leaving ours???

The flooding on South Indian Lake made our maps nearly worthless.

Everything looked different.

Our task was to find a small river leading out of South Indian Lake and into Moss Lake.

Finding small rivers like that is not always easy even with a <u>good</u> map and a <u>normal</u> lake. With the flooding, water ran *everywhere* making it look as if there could have been <u>dozens</u> of potential rivers.

We canoed over the tops of dead bushes trying to get a bearing on where we were. As frustration set in, the wind picked up, accompanied by 3 foot waves that were becoming dangerous.

After a lot of swearing, compass bearings, multiple passes along the shore line with aborted journeys into alleged rivers, we found it, but only by luck and perseverance.

Our reward when we finally got to Moss Lake was one of the worst campsites on the trip. We were now above the shield, and the water level was still high from the dam on South Indian Lake. This meant that the only campsite available was a small space surrounded by waterlogged trees.

That evening, the <u>rice</u> was once again a topic of discussion.

"All this rice is doing is adding weight to the canoe"

"Yeah, lets dump some of it, maybe the birds can digest it better than we can"

Since we had determined, with certainty, that the rice was coming out about the same way it went in, we decided to dump half of it. The rest we would be able to cook, and therefor, digest.

And as it turned out, it wouldn't be long before we were able to use the extra <u>calories</u> the cooked rice provided us. The next day we would be traveling <u>up</u> a small stream and into another watershed. As we rested that night, we knew from one of our maps that the route was "One Day of Hard Work."

This is an EXTREME understatement.

It should read, **"One of the Hardest Days of Your Life — <u>I'D TURN BACK IF I WERE YOU</u>!"**

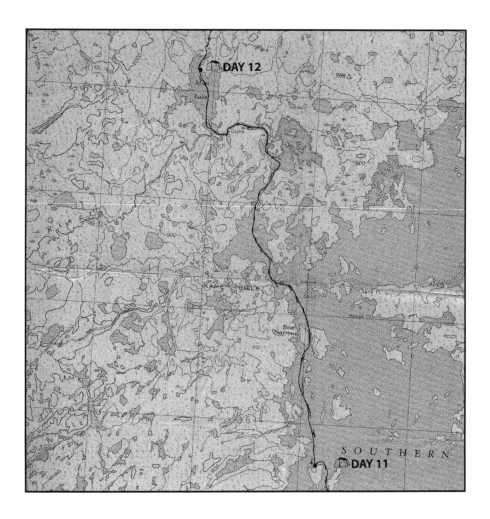

Day 13

Today we would travel <u>up</u> — *as in <u>against</u> the current* — Little Sand River and the first challenge of the day, once again, was <u>finding</u> it.

As on the day before, the shoreline was obscured by dead trees making river identification difficult. We finally just canoed into the trees on the most "river-like" waterway not really sure if we were on the right track or not.

The day was overcast with occasional rain. This, combined with the close proximity to the shore — *the "river" was only about 12 feet wide*

— brought out THE BUGS.

It was a nice change of pace to be on a small river after canoeing on huge lakes for so long, however, the presence of THE BUGS, ruined the effect.

Canoeing against the current was also giving us a workout.

And to make things even more interesting, the river never went straight for more than ten yards which was an additional pain-in-the-ass for the guy in the back doing the steering (me).

Special note — if you've ever had any formal canoe training, you know about the "J stroke" and other paddling techniques used to maneuver a typical canoe.

With our square stern version, however, those techniques were not nearly as effective and we had to invent new ones. The "hard lever" method — where you use the paddle as a lever and the side of the boat as a fulcrum, for example, was especially critical for fast turning in rapids. Out of necessity, we had taken the pretty looking "finesse" out of the sport and replaced it with down and dirty brute force.

At this point, we knew it was going to be a very hard day on the river, however, little did we know the wonders that would be around the next bend.

We approached the rapid with a lot of swearing.

It was obvious what we had to do — get out and drag the canoe up the rapid.

Tying a rope onto the bow, we attempted to drag the boat along the shoreline. This was not easy although we were making some progress.

Ahead was a slight obstacle — a sharp embankment with a tree sticking out of it. Fred was pulling the line upstream and I was holding the stern onto the shoreline.

Suddenly I heard a loud Shiiiiiit! and looked up to see Fred fall over, grab a sapling — *which immediately pulled out of the ground* — sending Fred splashing into the water.

It was actually quite humorous except that I knew that I was going to be the <u>next guy in</u> and moments later I found myself in the river along with Fred.

It was obvious what we had to do — <u>wade</u> the canoe up the rapid.

So now, with both of us totally soaked, we continued up the river.

"Hey Fred, Having fun yet?"

"Yeah, I hope there aren't too many more of those."

If all we had to do was drag a fully-loaded canoe up rapids in the rain with bugs all over our face it wouldn't have been so bad. But this river has an obstacle even more sinister than all of that <u>combined</u> — Log Jams.

The river was so small that when trees fall in — *and a lot do* — they eventually get stuck forming a dam which then collects more debris and becomes continually larger.

Then there was rampant <u>beaver mania</u>.

The stream must be a perfect habitat for beavers because, as we soon discovered, we were up against Super Beavers, and they were building the Hoover dams of the beaver world.

How to deal with a log jam and/or beaver dam

At this point, the shore consisted of quick sand and mud and portaging through that kind of muck is impossible. The only solution — *if you didn't think ahead and bring hand grenades* — was the following procedure…

Step 1 — Canoe up to the jam (ram the jam), while yelling "damn log jams" or "fucking beavers!" (depending on the type of obstacle) and grab something semi-stable (not easy to find) to keep from being sucked back down stream.

Step 2 — Get out and <u>balance on a floating log</u> while still <u>holding on to the canoe.</u>

Step 3 — Unload about 400lbs. of food and equipment and try to find a spot that will hold it all on the log/beaver jam.

Step 4 — Drag the canoe over the obstacle.

Step 5 — Reload the all the stuff (we were so tightly packed that loading and unloading was difficult enough on <u>dry</u> land; doing it on <u>floating logs</u> required true <u>talent</u>!).

Step 6 — Get back in and continue paddling <u>upstream</u>.

And guess what was around the next bend?

Maybe just a <u>rapid</u> for a change of pace!

This activity continued for such a long time that we were wondering if we were on the right river. We consulted the map but there were no landmarks to determine our position and we decided that even if we were on the *wrong* river it was too much work to go back. We would go wherever this leads, figure out where we are, and then deal with it. It had to come out <u>somewhere</u>!

Hours and hours went by. We were beyond exhausted. Camping on the river was out of the question because of THE BUGS and the quick sand and mud. We were determined to make it to a lake if it took all night.

And it almost did.

After struggling for 14 hours, we entered Sand Lake at about 11:00 pm.

It was a fitting conclusion that, being above the shield, there were <u>no</u> places to camp. There were dense trees and brush right up to the shoreline (who's idea was it to call it <u>Sand</u> Lake???).

So we moved on, finally spotting a clearing just big enough for the tent. Since there was no room for the canoe, we left it in the water, tied to a tree.

At that point, we were too tired to eat so we just passed out. THE BUGS were approaching unbearable. The campsite was in a cloud of mosquitoes and the woods hummed with their collective wing flapping and buzzing.

It's scary how <u>loud</u> they can get!

Day 14

The next day we were so exhausted that we only went a couple of miles, found a camp site that <u>did</u> have a sandy beach, and rested for the day.

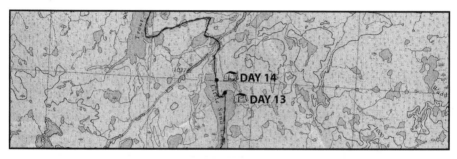

It was a nice day — warm and sunny, not much wind.

Unfortunately, this meant THE BUGS were so bad, we had to have our headnets on at all times.

Jeff shows off the latest trend in designer bug fashion. This matching set is functional, but still makes a statement.

Fred demonstrates the "bolted down look" which is very popular with people who do not have headnets.

We managed to clean up in the lake, but most of the day was spent trying to play guitar inside the tent, which was filled with dead bugs.

Playing guitar in a small two-man tent requires some new techniques as one person has to play while lying on his back.

Day 15

June 25, 1981. Today we would do a lot of portaging.

To get out of Sand Lake, we had to travel up (again) a very small stream. It was barely wider than the canoe with just enough water to float — most of the time.

We used our paddles to push along the banks since there wasn't enough room to get them in the water and — *when that didn't work* — we had to get out and push and wade.

We had a few portages to make and they were miserable, as portages always are unless, of course, you have a team of Himalayan Sherpas with you.

And THE BUGS were getting bad.

As the equipment was deposited at the end of the portage trail, it would attract THE BUGS and they would be waiting for us in increasing numbers on each subsequent trip (as you may recall, each portage required at least 3 trips to move all the stuff).

When we were ready to continue canoeing, THE BUGS would follow us onto the lake. Depending on the wind, it would take a while to ditch them.

At this point, THE BUGS were present 24 hours a day — black flies during the day and mosquitoes at night.

On the last portage of the day we found a dead snowmobile. The Indians use snowmobiles to travel and trap in the winter. I hope the owner of this one had a friend with him or he had a long, cold, walk home!

We almost blew it by taking the wrong stream into Trout Lake, but ultimately we managed to do the right thing, and were rewarded with an <u>ideal campsite</u>.

It was a small beach on an island in the middle of the lake and it was devoid of THE BUGS.

Small islands are usually good places to camp. There is not much chance of animals like bears and raccoons getting into your stuff!

The night was warm, and we were treated to a thunderstorm late in the evening.

Day 16

Trout Creek was the way out of Trout Lake and it was the Greek Ideal of a stream.

The water was crystal clear and the weather was sunny with no bugs. So we just relaxed and floated with the current, smoking joints along the way.

The creek lived up to its name, too. There were huge trout everywhere — probably could have reached out and grabbed one!

It began to get cloudy, windy, and rainy as we approached Chippewyan Lake.

We made camp near the mouth of the river that empties into the lake.

As soon as we got stoned, we were visited by a group from a fly-in fishing camp which consisted of a guide and some middle-aged white people.

The guide was very interested in our origins and our destination, however, THE BUGS, (which really weren't that bad) began to chew on the middle aged white folks and they wanted to go.

The guide invited us to their camp for coffee and fish, but being a few miles out of our way, we declined, although the strings of walleye they had caught made it almost look worth it!

Day 17

In the morning we awoke to THE BUGS and calm, but threatening, weather.

Afraid of getting windbound on Chippewyan Lake, and having no desire to hang out with THE BUGS, we ate and got out on the water in record time.

We made it across the lake and into the Seal River just as the wind picked up.

The Seal River provided more wind protection than an open lake, but at times it acted like a wind tunnel.

This was fun when the wind was at our backs as we would be flying down the river, but there were times when we were heading *into* the wind and it took all our strength to barely move.

At one point, we were forced to stop because of the weather, and had to pull onto a very small island.

Not knowing how long we would be stuck, we got stoned and ate granola.

> *"Not the ideal spot if this doesn't let up and we have to camp here"*

> *"We'll have to tie the boat up to a bush and sleep in it"*

> *"Great, let's smoke another bowl"*

The wind eventually died down enough to barely move so we gave it our all.

The effort was worth it because instead of sleeping in the canoe, tonight we would sleep in <u>real</u> beds!

We had stumbled upon the luxury accommodations of the wilderness — small shacks maintained by the Canadian Department of Hydrology. The area is apparently under study for another dam and crews are flown in periodically to collect data.

There were 3 tiny buildings in the hydrology complex. One was the size of an outhouse and contained the hydrology equipment.

Another building was for cooking and hanging out and equipped with a table, heater and stove The third was a small cabin with real beds and mattresses — we were in fat city!

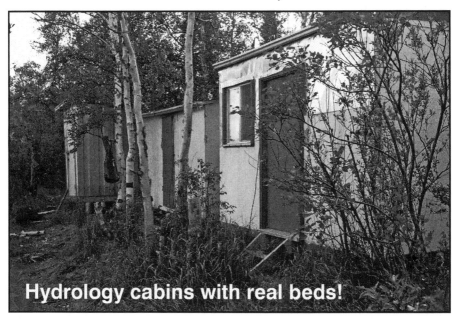

Hydrology cabins with real beds!

Day 18

Being tired of the hardships of living in a tiny tent, we decided to take the opportunity to hang out, play guitar, and <u>read the walls</u>.

> The walls of the eating cabin were covered with notes from hydrology teams and fellow travelers. Most described where they came from and where they were going, almost always being down the Seal River.
>
> One note mentioned that on November 1st it was 51 below.

Not finding any notes about people headed down the Caribou River we left a note that, after describing our origins and destination said, *"How come no one goes down the Caribou River? Is there something we don't know about?"*

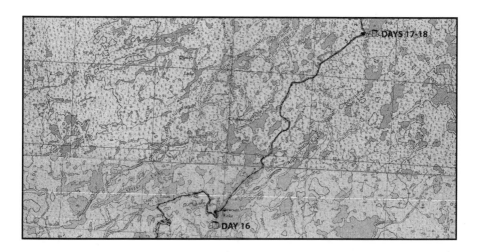

Day 19

The next day we had the wind at our backs and we would be facing some major rapids for the first time.

A prime concern of ours on this trip was not getting ourselves hurt or damaging the canoe — *it's a long walk home!* — so before we left, we had agreed that we would portage all rapids that looked the least bit <u>risky</u>.

It was with this attitude that we approached the first rapid marked on the map. We pulled over, put the canoe in park, and checked it out.

It was fairly innocuous — mostly fast water with a couple of boulders here and there. We put on our life jackets and shot right through.

The rest of the so-called "rapids" that were marked on the map were the same story. It was great fun. We would run through yelling "Free Ride" as we blasted down the center of the river.

After we had run <u>all</u> the rapids marked on the map with no problems we took off our life jackets and returned them to their normal duty as seat cushions.

"That's it. If all the rapids are like that we've got it made!"

"Hey, looks like a little more white water ahead — must not be much if it's not marked on the map."

74

We ran through the first set of unexpected rapids yelling "Free Ride" with no problem, rounded the bend, another set — *no problem* — one more set, "Free Ri... **looks like this one's runnin' over a boulder field and it's comin' up fast"** ... **CRAAAAASSHH!!!**

It <u>was</u> a boulder field all right, and we just hit one.

The worst had happened. The canoe flipped sideways, rapidly filled with water, and was pinned against the rock.

Fred and I found ourselves in rushing, <u>freezing</u> water over our heads *unsuccessfully* trying to keep our stuff, which was not tied in (but should have been!), from <u>floating out of the canoe</u> and down the river.

I yelled to Fred over the roar of the river...

"Did you save your paddle?"

"No"

"Take mine, can you take the canoe?"

"Yeah"

"I'll try to pickup some of the stuff"

We unpinned the canoe and Fred took it and some of the equipment.

I started swimming down the gushing rapid as fast as possible to catch up with a pack, 2 guitars, a paddle, the tent, one food bag, both day packs, the map, and a few other odds and ends.

What an interesting feeling to see most of your stuff go floating down a river in the middle of nowhere!

To catch up to the stuff, I had to swim *faster* than the current and avoid hitting any <u>body-breaking</u> boulders.

The river was quickly sucking the energy out of me as I started grabbing some of the stuff. The more I retrieved, the more I got weighed down and the harder it was to swim. I was breathing as hard as I could while trying not to inhale any of the violent water that was rampaging around me.

Fortunately, I managed to catch up with *almost* everything except the tent, my daypack, and some little stuff.

The other good news was, my backpack floated so well that it helped keep me up. The major problem now, was hypothermia. I was losing heat fast enough in the freezing water that I was now in serious danger of drowning.

I focused all my strength on heading to shore with all I could carry.

Meanwhile, Fred was upstream with the canoe, his pack, and one of the food packs.

He had managed to unload the remaining stuff, empty the canoe of water, reload it, successfully negotiate the rest of the rapid, and show up just in time to retrieve the floating items I had collected, and me.

I was so cold I couldn't stop shaking, so after catching up to the tent and a few other items, we found a campsite and hung out the stuff to dry.

Drying out after the crash

Broken Canoe

There was a broken canoe up in the trees...
looks like someone didn't make it,
hope they had more than one canoe!

We were lucky we were alive and the crash damage wasn't too bad.

Damage Report

Lost...

    1 back pack cover
    1 fiber pile jacket
    1½ pairs of hiking boots
    1 mosquito head net
    1 fish net
    1 shirt
    1 pair of rain pants
    1 sock

Damaged...

    Watch ceased to function
    Rip in space blanket
    Nasty but repairable dents in the canoe

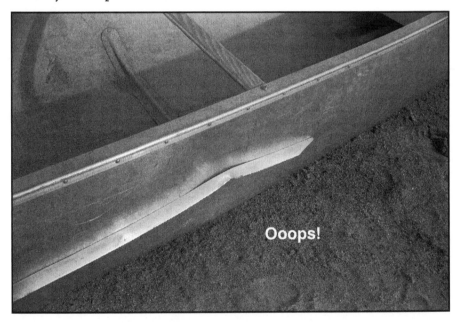

After settling down a bit — *and warming up* — we climbed an esker, got stoned, and were treated to a nice view of the surrounding area.

View from an esker

Fred at the top of an esker

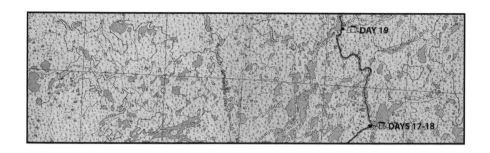

Day 20

We canoed the rest of the Seal River cautiously. If it looked at all like a rapid we got out and waded, and we no longer trusted *any* of the maps.

> *A word about the maps... We carried two types of maps. The topographical maps, which you see in this book, were made in the 1950s. On these maps, the major features like lakes and rivers are accurately shown except when a dam has been installed in later years like it was on South Indian Lake.*
>
> *Minor features, like the location of rapids, were also shown on the topo maps leading us to believe the map was accurately made, but it wasn't. Some of the worst areas of rapids are not shown, and many of the marked rapids were simply fast water and no big deal to run in a canoe. Bottom line is, although they were the "official topos," these maps could not be trusted.*
>
> *The second set of maps were sold to us by the Manitoba Department of Tourism, Recreation, and Cultural Affairs. They had what appeared to be detailed descriptions of the canoe routes like, "dangerous rapid here, portage 150 paces to left of the big boulder" but they also turned out to be inaccurate.*
>
> *As we later learned, these maps were intended to be "art" and promotional tools for tourism rather than guide maps. It would have been nice if the people who sold us the maps let us know that when we first acquired them, so we wouldn't have based life or death decisions on bad information, but they didn't.*

OK, back to life on the Seal...

The further we proceeded down the river, the more intense the whitewater became.

The porcupine rapids, which have a degree of notoriety, were pretty wild looking and about a quarter mile long.

Portaging the rapids in most cases wasn't a practical alternative to running them. They were too long, we had too much stuff, and the river banks were not conducive to foot travel.

So getting out and <u>wading</u> the canoe down the sides of the river with ropes tied to the canoe was the method we used most often.

Wading through the rapids, however, was no fun and not all that <u>safe</u> either.

Not knowing what the bottom of the river is like, we would find ourselves over our heads and out of control or getting slammed into boulders by a fully-loaded 400-pound canoe powered by rushing water.

Our shins and knees were the big losers in this activity.

After seemingly *endless* miles of rapids, we reached the mouth of the Seal River where we camped.

Before us was Tadule Lake.

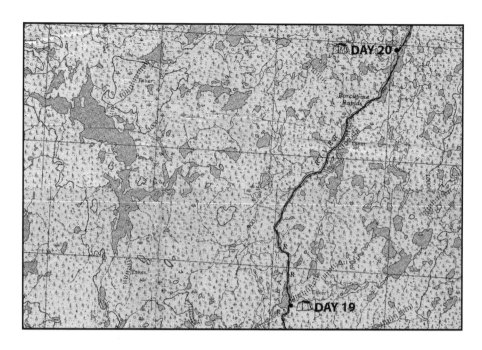

Trying to make sure we didn't hit any more boulders!

Tadule Lake - The Turning Point

Day 21

The next morning there were Indians wandering around our camp. This time, we didn't even bother getting out of the tent, we just went back to sleep.

When we woke up later, we ate cereal and broke camp.

As we entered Tadule Lake, it was quite foggy. Canoeing in the fog is a mystical experience so we got stoned.

Tadule Lake is <u>huge</u> and dotted with hundreds of small islands. The fog made everything seem extraordinarily erie, but the enveloping silence was eventually broken by a wicked wind.

We found an Island and camped.

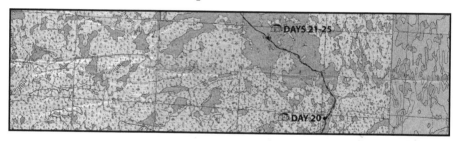

Days 22-25

It was our intention to hang out for a while before we hit the big time canoe route — <u>up</u> the Wolverine River, and <u>down</u> the Caribou. The island we found seemed like a good place to take a break as it had one major thing going for it — no BUGS.

The weather also turned miraculously nice — 75 degrees and sunny!

Things seemed to be going our way.

Tadule Lake

Our island hanging out activities consisted of, as usual, drinking coffee, getting stoned, and playing guitar. Not really much else to do in the woods, except entertain an occasional guest.

Tadule Lake Campsite

Our third day of hanging out was the Fourth of July. To celebrate, we drank the last of the coffee and shot off one of the firecrackers we had brought to scare off the polar bears.

We also celebrated that the next day we would be off to the Tadule Lake Indian Village to get more coffee.

At least we <u>thought</u> we would be off to the Indian Village, but the next day the wind was at gale force and we were windbound again.

This time, it was a good test for the tent.

My tent is a Stephenson's Warmlite, known for its radical design, durability, and light weight (3.5 lbs). It allegedly withstands 90-mile-per-hour winds. I don't think we had any 90-mile-per-hour winds, but I am sure the gusts were hitting 60.

Since our fingers were too raw to play guitar and the coffee was gone, we spent most of the day trying to keep the tent from blowing away.

Day 26

July 6, 1981. Today was to be totally horrible.

The wind subsided — <u>completely</u>. We broke camp and headed out on the water where we were greeted by the most incredible <u>cloud of</u>

gnats on the face of the earth.

Everything was covered solid with gnats. Our brightly colored packs were now grey from the density of THE BUGS. The ones that couldn't find a spot on our equipment covered our bodies and formed a dense cloud around the canoe. They were using our faces as an air strip, too, continuously landing and taking off.

I was in the back and could hardly see Fred through THE BUGS. In addition to the gnats, there were about 20 Deer Flies that were doing figure eights around us.

This may sound like an exaggeration, but I assure you it is not.

At least the lack of wind made for easy paddling, and the prospect of replenishing our coffee supply at the Indian settlement kept our spirits up!

However, when we arrived at the area where the town was *supposed* to be, we found no town. So we paddled around. Still no town. We were definitely in the right spot according to the map, so we concluded that either there was no town or it was somewhere else.

So we paddled on, along with our BUG escort.

It was a fairly long haul to the top of the lake where Tadule empties into Negassa lake via a large rapid. Being quite tired and not wanting to deal with a rapid, we looked for a camp site.

The shoreline, however, was not cooperative. It was very steep with trees everywhere. The only spot where camping was at all possible was an area about the size of our tent and it was by no means flat.

The water in this area was moving quickly towards the rapid. Having learned our hydrology lessons well, we rammed the shore and quickly yanked the canoe out of the water, our cloud of BUGS still intact.

But the MIX OF BUGS had changed. We suddenly realized that the bug cloud was no longer just gnats, but THE DREADED BLACK FLIES and they began to bite.

In a state of panic, we pulled all the stuff from the canoe and began to make camp. It was the fastest I've ever put the tent together — a true Olympian performance. I would have gotten perfect tens, except that I evidently did not have one of the poles exactly right because when I pulled the tent tight — Snap!

We had broken a pole. Score that perfect zeros — lots of <u>bugs</u> and no <u>house</u>.

While being severely attacked by the unrelenting black flies, I dug through my pack, found the duct tape, mended the pole, and this time successfully erected the tent.

Meanwhile, Fred had secured the canoe and the rest of the equipment. We dove in the tent and began the task of killing all THE BUGS that came in with us. This would take about half an hour.

Having eradicated all THE BUGS, we proceeded to get stoned.

"What a pleasant end to a nice day"

"Do you hear something in the distance — like a motorboat?"

The sound grew louder and louder and our fears were confirmed — somebody was stopping by and we would have to go out into THE BUGS.

Two Indians pulled up. We talked while <u>walking around real fast</u> and <u>waving our arms</u> at THE BUGS.

It was a bit of an intense experience, however, two extremely valuable pieces of information were obtained from the Indians...

1. THE BUGS are <u>worse</u> where we were going ~ *and* ~

2. The real location of the Indian Village

The Indians left and we dove back in the tent and killed all of THE BUGS again.

Being in the tent was not much better than the bug cloud. The tent was pitched at a 45 degree angle which made both sitting and lying down difficult.

Due to the design of my sleeping bag, I was unable to inflate my air mattress because I would slide downhill. Therefore, I had to sleep directly on the ground which was cold and rocky.

Fred used the opportunity to bring up the fact that the trip had started to be less fun than originally advertised.

"THE BUGS are unbearable here how can they be worse up north?"

"I'm not too anxious to find out."

"Going up the Wolverine is going to be a royal bitch. We might not make it to Hudson Bay on time."

"If we could get a message to John Hicks we could go down the Seal. That would shave off about 100 miles and 2 weeks. And at least we know its possible to canoe it."

"That's the river Harry's friend got killed on."

"Yeah."

So it was decided. We wanted the quickest way out and that was the Seal River. If the Indian Village could contact John Hicks, the guy we had hired to pick us up on Hudson Bay, we could do it. It was worth a try.

That night it rained and, because of the angle, the tent leaked through the floor.

We got soaked.

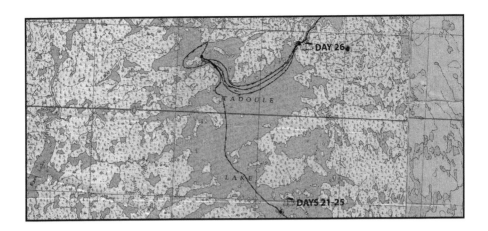

Day 27

The next day we canoed back to the <u>real</u> location of the Indian Village. Distance is gained by so much effort it felt bad to go backwards, but the possibility of shortening the trip, as well as scoring some more <u>coffee</u>, made it worth the attempt.

Along the way we found a group of fellow voyagers camped on some rocks. In conformance with wilderness etiquette, we stopped.

They were from Minnesota and were on their second trip in the area.

On the first trip, they had gone down the Seal River. This time, they were going to try to get to the Thelwiaza river and then try to canoe the Bay to Churchill. This was the same route Harry Stimson had tried. We told them what he had said about the river with no water. They didn't seem to care and were determined to try it anyway.

Still on their first week out, they were fresh and full of enthusiasm. Starting from South Indian Lake, they had also taken the supply boat, however, the boat people charged them 100 dollars! When we told them we got a ride for free, they flipped.

We also told them we were tired of lots of bugs and no beer and asked them about the Seal River. They told us there were intense rapids all the way. Especially dangerous were Canyon Rapids. They said that we wouldn't make it in our canoe, which was reassuring (as you may recall, our canoe was designed for use with a motor, not for shooting dangerous rapids, or really, *any* rapids at all).

Continuing on to the Indian Village, we could see some cabins in the distance.

As we got closer, we could see children running to the shore to greet us. Some adults came down, too. Apparently a visitation is a major event.

Pulling onto the shore, we greeted everyone. I felt like an old world explorer discovering some lost colony.

Explaining our situation, and our desire to alter our route and pick up arrangements on Husdon Bay, we were referred to Sam, the Chief's nephew, who had a radio.

We found Sam. He invited us to his cabin, and over coffee, he told us flat out that we would not make it down the Caribou River.

He had traveled that river during winter in a snowmobile, and from his description, the caribou is one continuous rapid through a canyon, all the way to Hudson Bay. Bottom line was, nobody goes down the Caribou River in a canoe. The *only* way out was the Seal River.

Sam said he had grown up with John Hicks, the guy who was supposed to pick us up. He would radio him and tell him to pick us up at the mouth of the Seal River in two weeks.

Because the radio reception was bad that day, Sam was unable to reach Churchill and John Hicks, but he said he would get through sometime in the next week. He told us to go to the cabin at the north end of the Seal River and that's where we would be picked up. He also said camping on the bay without a gun was extremely risky because of the polar bears.

Having made our arrangements, we celebrated by going to the town store for some coffee. The store, however, was no supermarket and there was no instant coffee. But, they did have maple buds (a candy) which we ate for immediate gratification. We were also able to pick up some dried food and pepper to add to the rice which we had been eating boiled and plain.

The rest of the day, we played with the kids and checked out the rest of the town.

> Tadule Lake Village was formed in the early 1970s and consists of about 100 acres of cleared land with a dozen or two small cabins, a town store, and a building with a generator in it. The tribe had formerly lived in Churchill, but they were on welfare and alcohol. The Chief and the Canadian Government arranged to put them on Tadule Lake which is two weeks of hard and dangerous canoeing to the nearest beer. Only the Chief has a small plane. Supplies are brought in once a year on a DC3 that lands on the ice. Satellite TV was rumored to be coming the following year.

The 6 other canoers we had met earlier had also come to town.

They were surprised that we had pulled up our canoe with all our stuff in it and just left it on the beach. They had hidden all their stuff at their camp which is quite unnecessary. To think that someone would steal your stuff in the middle of the wilderness is absurd. The Indians living in civilization may be drunk and obnoxious, but in our experience, the ones in the woods are some of the finest people on the planet and would do just about anything to <u>help</u> you.

We told the canoers from Minnesota our new plans. They were aware of the cabin on Hudson Bay. One of them said that his sister had stayed there and a polar bear broke down the front door sending them running out the back.

They also knew of someone who had their tent ripped up by bears.

They also re-expressed their doubts about us making it down the Seal River with our type of canoe and no spray covers.

That evening we made an attempt to follow them to their camp, as we were invited to join them, but the wind and waves were so strong we couldn't keep up with them in our fully-loaded, non-expedition style canoe. And without "spray covers," we were getting swamped by the waves.

We headed for the nearest island.

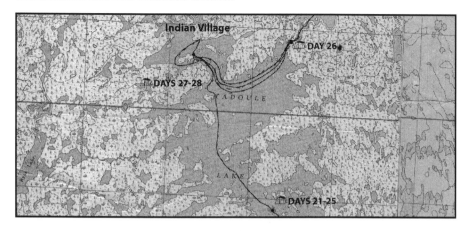

The trees are starting to thin out

Day 28

The next day we were windbound again. All attempts to canoe out of the island had failed. At this point we had a tight schedule to keep, and being windbound was a major cause for concern, but there was absolutely nothing we could do about it.

Cooking rice

Windbound again, but Fred tries to
stay in shape by canoeing on the sand

Day 29

The following day was just as windy, but to our delight, the wind had switched to the direction we wanted to go.

The problem now, was that the waves were dangerously high and it looked liked rain, however, we just plain ol' didn't give a shit, and didn't want to risk getting <u>stuck</u> for any longer.

We loaded up and pushed off.

The wind and waves laid into the boat. It took a great deal of strength to keep on course, but we <u>were</u> moving forward.

Heading out of the bay, we entered the open water of the huge lake. The waves were now 3-4 feet high and there was stormy-looking gloom rapidly approaching, but there was no turning back now.

Suddenly we found ourselves in the middle of a violent thunderstorm. Our visibility was cut to zero, and our concentration turned to staying afloat while we debated the consequences of being in an aluminum canoe in the middle of a lake with lots of lightning.

The storm passed.

We took on a good amount of water, but didn't sustain any damage.

After the storm, the waves were still big and a problem to deal with.

I was in the back of the canoe, and as I looked behind me, right before a wave would hit us, all I could see was a wall of water. At times, the water was so shallow in the troughs between waves we would nearly bottom out. Then, as the wave passed *under* the canoe, it would lift up and both the bow and stern would be exposed. Then we would sink into another trough and repeat the cycle.

My <u>steering</u> job was to counteract the action of the waves which tended to turn us broadside. Turning broadside would immediately <u>sink</u> us. <u>All</u> of our canoeing efforts were used in maintaining the right angle to avoid <u>sinking</u>. Any forward motion was solely compliments of the wind and waves.

The big lakes...
sometimes they can be calm (as shown here)
and sometimes violent (as described above)

We finally made it back to the top of Tadule Lake and were greeted by a series of rapids, so it was get out and wade time.

The water was cold.

Along the way, we ran into the group we had met at the Indian village. They were pulling out Arctic Grayling as fast as they could throw the line into the water.

Grayling are neat fish. When first pulled out of the water, they are exquisitely rainbow colored. Then they quickly fade to gray.

Our fellow adventurers offered us some fish and gave us a few more pointers such as, *"the next rapids you come across are some of the worst on the trip"* and *"you can't canoe canyon rapids with that canoe, you'll have to portage"* along with, *"watch out if you get lucky and happen to make it to the end of the river alive — the last rapids are the worst."*

We thanked them for the good news and pressed on.

They were the last people we would see for a <u>long</u> time.

To Hudson Bay

Negassa Lake was smaller and therefore not as wavy. The wind was still ferocious though, making crossing it exhausting.

At the mouth of the river leading from Negassa to Shethanei Lake, the water began to pick up momentum fast.

We hurried to shore to get a look at what we were getting ourselves into.

It was a rapid all right — about a half mile of frothy churning water just waiting to mangle a canoe. This was going to be a bitch. Running it was totally out of the question. Wading it was also questionable. Portaging would be way too much effort and was definitely out of the question.

The work began... pulling, dragging — *water up to the chest* — getting slammed into boulders while fighting a raging current.

After a long struggle, we *almost* made it to the end, but found ourselves in the <u>middle</u> of the river clinging to a boulder with <u>nowhere to go</u>.

The water was over our heads and to our side was the most incredible wall of rushing water I had ever seen. The roar was so loud we couldn't hear each other. Using hand signals to communicate, we ventured out slowly while hanging onto the rock.

Suddenly, the current was too strong and violently ripped us off the rock.

We were immediately sucked into the main rapid clutching on to our canoe.

The ride was wild, quick, and to the point — straight down the chute. No boulders. No smashed knees. We just shot right into Shethanei Lake like we were on some mega ride in a waterpark. What fun!

We climbed aboard the canoe, rested for a minute, and bailed out the water.

As soon as we found a good spot we, camped and got stoned.

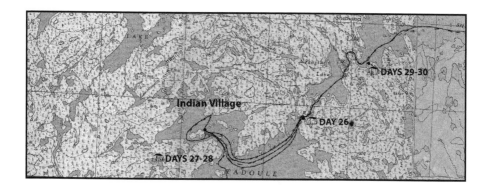

Day 30

The next day we awoke to the sound of wind. It was back, and it was coming from the wrong direction. We were windbound again.

It was a good day for experiments. We were entering peak season for black flies and were wondering, as you might be now, just how many black flies are there?

Well, you wouldn't want to go outside in your underwear. In fact, you wouldn't want to go outside unless you had every conceivable spot of skin <u>sealed off</u>.

Even then, the black flies would find a way to crawl down your gators, up your pants, and down your socks just to bite you in the ankles and give you something to remember your vacation by.

So, you probably wouldn't want to go out at all. However, life must go on and it is necessary to go outside, and every time this was done, <u>millions</u> of black flies would enter the tent necessitating a hunt.

Actually "millions" <u>is</u> an over statement of the truth, but one time when I left the tent, Fred decided to count the flies as he killed them.

The door was open all of 3-4 seconds.

The official total — 144.

> Black flies, of course, are legendary in the far North and much has been written about them. The truth is, no matter how many stories you read, or how long someone talks about it, the

intensity of THE BUGS must be experienced to be believed.

And there is no escape. The bugs are present 24 hours a day, with black flies prevalent during the daytime and mosquitoes at night. They can be thick enough to cloud the sky (and your tent screens!), and they can, and have, caused death in people and animals.

Bug repellent, by the way, doesn't work very well in those conditions.

Watching the bugs eat Fred (next image)

The joy of Black Flies

Fred uses the calming waters to practice the ancient discipline of Black Fly Zen

Day 31

The wind died down the next morning and we were off.

Shetlanie Lake is extremely beautiful and very long.

The problem we were facing now, was that we seemed to have damaged the canoe in the last series of rapids and were slowly sinking. This required us to stop and bail out the canoe every 15 minutes or so. With 120 miles to go, this could prove to be quite irritating and somewhat dangerous — the canoe was difficult enough to maneuver without water sloshing around inside.

We had lunch on a sandy beach near an esker.

For some reason, the bugs weren't too bad. Taking the break-from-the-bugs opportunity, we pulled all the stuff out of the canoe so we could find the leak.

A little geyser emanating from the bottom of the canoe pointed out the problem immediately — we had popped a rivet.

Now what?

Well, although we neglected to bring spray covers — *not wanting our guitars to be out of commission on the trip* — we <u>did</u> bring a variety of spare parts including guitar pegs.

So, one <u>guitar peg</u> jammed in the popped rivet hole and we were sea worthy again!

As we came to the end of Shethanei Lake, we entered the Seal River which was to be the last great leg in our journey.

There are about 65 sets of rapids we would have to negotiate on the Seal River and the river didn't waste any time getting started, although the first few rapids were an easy run.

We canoed all the way to the mouth of the Wolverine River that day.

The Wolverine was the river we were originally going to take to get to the Caribou River.

We camped at the mouth of it and gave thanks that we did <u>not</u> have to canoe it. We would have had to go <u>upstream</u>, and we could see a nice set of rapids that were there to greet any traveler.

Its hard enough to get <u>down</u> a rapid.

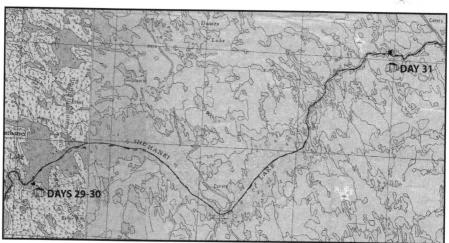

Day 32

There was apprehension in the air as we woke. Today we would have to face many rapids, and tomorrow, we would challenge the legendary rapids of Great Island.

We were anxious to see if we would live through this, so we wasted no time in getting going.

The weather was miserable — cold and rainy. THE BUGS were out in full force. The rapids were intense. We got so wet that if we stopped to rest, we would start shaking from hypothermia and get attacked by THE BUGS.

If we canoed, we had to face life threatening rapids.

What a choice!

Lunch time was a real treat. We came across the worst rapid we had seen so far. The problem was, we couldn't figure out how to get though it or around it without getting killed. So we pulled up on some rocks and ate lunch instead.

A huge storm was approaching.

As we ate our granola, we could see the storm approach with a view of the worst part of the rapids in the foreground. Behind us was a huge cloud of black flies waiting for the wind to die down so they could attack us.

We ate until hypothermia made us start shaking. At that point, we had no choice but to <u>do something</u>. We dragged the canoe over a bunch of rocks, roped up the stuff and did some rock climbing with the canoe.

After much hard work, we cleared the <u>death</u> portion of the rapid without mishap.

It was a two joint evening.

The Stephenson Warmlite Tent

There's no place like home

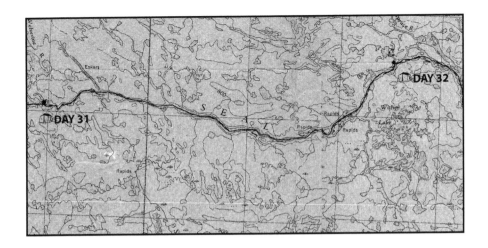

Day 33

This was it. Today we would face the legendary rapids of Great Island.

At Great Island, the river forks and runs through narrow passages increasing the speed of the flow of the river. This creates some nasty rapids. Anyone we talked to about this river mentioned these rapids and especially the Canyon Rapids.

The Island itself has a history, something about Indians meeting White People a long time ago. We, however, did not want to become a permanent part of its history.

At the fork in the river, we took the passage to the right. It was supposed to be the route with the least chance of getting ground up. We hit rapids immediately. Ran some, waded some. No problem.

With all the action, it was difficult to track our position on the map or know how far we had gone. Consequently, we were always on the lookout for "canyon rapids."

Suddenly, the shoreline rose into a <u>wall</u> and the water picked up speed.

In front of us was a boulder field with water running over it. Since the walls on both sides of the river were quite high, it was impossible to pull over and check it out.

Were we entering canyon rapids?

If we were, we had no choice but to run it full speed and hope for the best.

The pace of the river quickened and the boulders came up faster and faster. It took teamwork and concentration to miss them all. The job of the person in front was to spot the boulders and yell, *"boulder right!"* or *"hard left — fast!!!"* The job of the person in the back was to make sure we missed them all.

If we got <u>too</u> close to a boulder without time to maneuver, the person in front would have to slam the boulder with the paddle to avoid a collision.

In this respect, our canoe paddles, made by Carlise, really saved our lives.

They were constructed of some indestructible plastic and were one of the outstanding pieces of equipment from a performance perspective.

A lesser paddle would have left us stranded and probably dead.

Meanwhile, back to the river. After a 1/2 mile wild, fast-water ride, not knowing if we were going to go over a waterfall, run death rapids or what, the river slowed down, and the good news was, we were still afloat.

Canyon Rapids, however, were still ahead of us.

We could hear the <u>roar</u> as we rounded the bend.

Then we could see it. It was awesome and brought on that "holy shit" feeling.

We quickly landed on a small beach. If this *wasn't* canyon rapids, I couldn't imagine what could be worse, short of Niagra Falls.

Fred and I split up to look for the portage route. He checked out the area upstream.

Walking downstream, I found what looked like a portage trail heading up a steep cliff. I was thinking about what a rough portage this was going to be as I climbed upward.

111

The path brought me to the top of the canyon wall. Below, I could see the rapid and paused to admire its ferocity. Anxious to find a way *around* the deadly waters, I continued down the path which was suddenly cut off by another canyon. The drop was about 100 feet and the side canyon continued as far as I could see.

Unless Fred had found something, there was no way to portage this rapid.

I stopped back at the view of the rapid with a different perspective. I realized that our chances of <u>not</u> making it through were much greater than making it.

But there had to be one route through the rapid that was less risky than the others so I studied the situation. It is a scene I will never forget.

I was also thinking about how far it was to Hudson Bay if we lost the canoe and had to walk. And what if we broke our legs?

I returned to the canoe. Fred returned shortly thereafter.

"Did you find a route?"

"No, did you?"

"No"

"Did you see the rapid from up on the cliff?"

"Yeah — I don't think our chances are real good runnin' this thing. What if we try to get around this island? Can't be any worse on the other side."

The main part of the rapid was clearly visible from the top of the canyon wall and we agreed on a strategy if we got caught in the main part of it.

But our only <u>real</u> hope was a channel on the other side of the river where it forked to go around a small island. Although we couldn't see what was on the other side of the island, it couldn't be any worse than what we could see from the side of the river we were on.

It was certainly worth a chance, and I'll take hope over nearly guaranteed death.

The immediate problem was getting <u>across</u> the river without getting sucked down the middle and into the large, deadly rapid we could see.

With our decision made, I decided against returning to the cliff for pictures — the <u>black flies</u> had found us.

And that would compound the difficulties. Since mosquito netting cuts visibility too much, we would now have to run this thing with black flies all over our face.

Heading out into the river, we paddled up stream a bit, and then headed across. About 1/3 the way into the river, the current grabbed us good.

We paddled for all we were worth but the rapids approached at greater and greater speed. The adrenaline flowed in quantities hereto unknown, but the effort seemed futile... it looked like we would be carried down the death part of the rapid — broadside!

But we weren't dead yet, and the unwillingness to die on a stupid canoe trip finally pushed us those extra yards just in time.

We made it to where the river branches off to go around the far side of the island and got instantly slammed against a rock wall. The water was moving quickly, but there were no major obstacles in sight.

We found a small ledge, got out, and roped the canoe. A cliff rose high above us. Using our rock climbing skills, we inched our way along. Rounding a bend, we could see a <u>wall of white water</u> in front of us. We weren't out of this one yet. In fact, we appeared to be <u>trapped</u>.

We continued to the end of the passage where the two parts of the river reunited in a huge wall of white water. There seemed to be no way to enter the river from where we were.

I climbed up over some rock outcroppings at the end of the island.

On the other side of the rock wall I could see a possible launch site. The problem was getting the canoe there.

Fred hauled the stuff up and handed it to me. Now for the canoe. Fred threw me the bow rope and gradually let out the stern until the river grabbed the canoe. It yanked the rope out of his hands and whipped it — *whipped it good* — against some rocks.

No damage. Lucky... again.

We got the canoe in position to launch, loaded it back up, and planned our run. The objective was to head for the calm waters that we could see ahead.

But first, we had to negotiate around a series of boulders the size of dump trucks with walls of frothy water screaming around them.

We launched. It was a white-knuckle paddle run that took us within inches of the aforementioned giant boulders at high velocity, but we made it.

And they said it couldn't be done!!!

The rest of the day continued in the same vein, although after our experiences at Canyon Rapids, we became callous to danger. We just did whatever we had to do to stay afloat.

The last series of Great Island rapids seemed endless, but we just kept moving forward like a non-stop rapid-eating machine.

Yes, we had turned into — Canoeing Zombies!

Eventually, we reached quiet water at the end of Great Island and found ourselves camped on an island, getting stoned in the tent, laughing hysterically at the day's events, and feeling satisfied that we were ever closer to <u>steaks and beer</u>.

Rapids on the Seal River

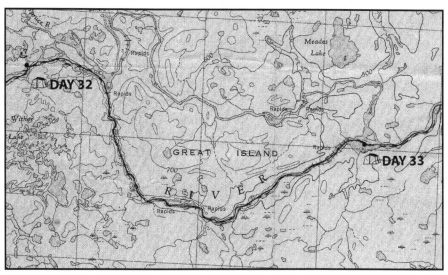

Days 34-35

The days on the Seal River were now becoming routine.

It was almost like a job.

Upon waking, we would look up at the tent and see that it was totally covered with mosquitoes.

Mosquitoes on the tent.
They are actually thining out
just before the black flies take over.

Early morning, evening,
and "night" the mosquitoes are
solid on the screen so you can't see out. No kidding.

One of us would have to go outside to make breakfast and both of us would have to take a shit. As I mentioned earlier in this story, "speed shitting" is a critical skill when you're dealing with bugs of this magnitude.

The idea is to wait until it is practically hanging out your ass. Then run out of the tent, pull down your pants, and smack mosquitoes while you plop it down. During wiping, of course, it's harder to swat mosquitoes. All in all you would receive about fifty bites right away and there would always be a few bugs left in your pants that you'd have to get later.

After breakfast, it was time to put on the wet set of clothes for wading and running rapids. There was no way to dry clothes out over night, so we stored the wet set in the back of the tent. Putting them back on in the morning would instantly drop your body temperature a few degrees.

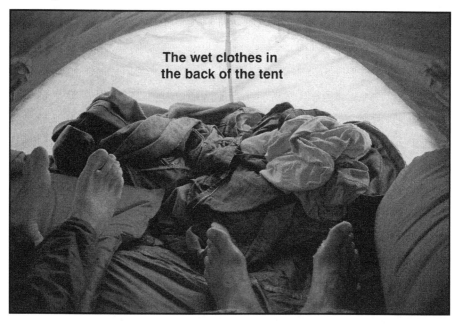

The wet clothes in the back of the tent

Then there was the see-how-fast-you-can-break-camp contest. With all those BUGS, I'm sure we set some records!

The main event, of course, was onto the river to face life threatening rapids all day.

We had an almost-vaporized experience at least once or twice a day.

For example, one time we missed a boulder the size of a Volkswagen by a few inches.

Another time we took the middle of the river, since there weren't supposed to be any rapids according to the map. Suddenly, we noticed that there were rapids on <u>both</u> sides of us and in front of us were four foot high standing waves.

In this case, the last thing I heard was Fred saying was, *"Oh Shit"* (he was in the front of the canoe).

117

The next thing I knew, we were crashing through a series of sizable standing waves that were causing large volumes of water to fall on my lap.

"Bail, Bail — next time we'll bring spray covers!"

It took some <u>fast</u> action to get the canoe bailed out enough to maneuver the <u>next</u> set of rapids that were quickly approaching.

Although we were running more and more difficult rapids, we still were doing our fair share of wading. Better to wade a little than to have to walk a lot (an old Indian Proverb we found etched in a rock).

After a days work, we would make camp as fast as possible, get stoned, laugh about the days activities, and eat dinner (at this point, we were too tired, and there were too many bugs to cook rice, so we just ate granola).

Oh yeah, about the "<u>days</u> work." We never really knew how long that was because my watch — *the only one we had* — was wiped out when we crashed the canoe earlier in the trip. And the sun is always about the same in this area at this time of year — *day and night* — so it's hard to keep track of time or even know for sure what day it is.

The Seal River

Despite the craziness, there were many beautiful moments, too.

As to be expected on the <u>Seal</u> River, we were followed by seals most of the way. They were as curious about us as we were of them. They would sneak up about 5 feet from the boat and pop their heads out. When we made eye contact, they would dive underwater, swim out 20 yards or so, and pop their heads out again.

At one point, there were about a dozen seals surrounding us.

Seals on the Seal River

Being on the edge of the tundra, the trees were almost non-existent and the ones that were surviving were pretty scrawny.

Another tell-tale sign that we were in the far north was seeing snow banks along the river in mid July.

Fred sits on a snow bank in mid July

As we continued down the Seal towards Hudson Bay, the trees started thinning out even more. We had gone from the Land of Little Sticks, to the Land of Littlest Sticks, and soon, we would be in the Land of <u>No</u> Sticks!

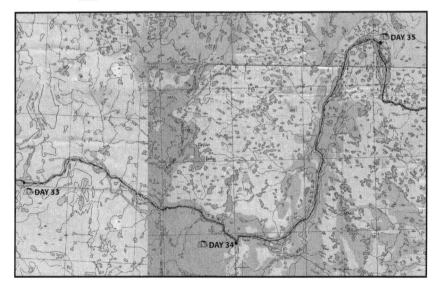

Almost Tundra

Day 36

Since we had been making good progress down the Seal River — *shooting rapids has one advantage, and that is, <u>speed</u>* — we decided to hang out at a cabin that was indicated on the map as being a few miles before the mouth of the Seal River.

This would limit the time we would have to face the polar bears.

After a hard 10–14 hours of rapid running, we came to the area where the cabin was supposed to be and, of course, it either did not exist or was in a different location.

Since the cabin on the bay — *the one we were to be picked up at* — was supposedly "just north of the mouth of the Seal," and seemingly not all that far from where we currently were, we decided to go for it.

The map showed that the Seal river turned into a delta about a half mile wide.

<u>No</u> rapids were indicated. It looked like easy paddling from here on. Just a lazy delta like on the good ol' Mississippi.

Yeah, right... as the river widened, the pace of the water began to pick up speed. We hit a rapid, and as we continued, the water started running faster and faster and branching out in all directions around small islands and large boulders.

The river had also widened to the point where the banks were no longer in sight, which meant that we didn't know where we were or which way to go.

We only knew that if we went the same direction as the water we would end up in the ocean... but <u>when</u>?

We were already so tired, we didn't want to stop for <u>anything</u>. Not even to check out the rapids, which would have been difficult anyway, since there weren't many places to land the canoe.

On this day, I was in the back. Spotting a rough looking spot ahead I asked Fred if we should check it out.

"Looks OK," he said just before we crashed over a three foot waterfall and zig zagged between a bunch of boulders.

We laughed and continued to run everything in sight.

To add to the experience, the delta area must be a breading ground for sea gulls. In the spirit of protecting their young, they were flying at us and jumping on our heads. We fought them off with our paddles. If we weren't so busy running rapids, we would have stopped for omelets.

It felt like we had been canoeing <u>forever</u> down rapids, smashing into boulders, and going over small waterfalls.

The canoe was getting the shit beat out of it.

And so were we. It was like canoeing in a big pinball machine and we were scoring lots of points bouncing from boulder to boulder.

"Where's the fuckin' Bay?"

No sign of it.

"Where the hell are we?"

More rapids.

Eventually, we arrived at a somewhat level area and pulled the canoe onto a rock. There <u>was</u> something in the breeze... a slight change of environment, I could <u>smell</u> it — *salt water!*

And barely visible on the horizon was a large blue patch — the Arctic Ocean!

Unfortunately, the blue was far beneath us. We still needed to drop some altitude, and that meant <u>more rapids</u>.

We continued running everything that came our way without giving it a second thought.

Until one.

"Better check this one out," we agreed. And then, <u>silence</u> as we pulled up to an overwhelming sight with humble reverence and respect.

This must have been where Harry Stimson's friend got killed. We remembered that the canoers we met on Tadule Lake said the last rapid was the worst. Hopefully, that meant this <u>WAS</u> the last rapid we would have to deal with.

Fortunately, were able to wade the boat along the side of this rapid without much difficulty. A few feet away, however, endless amounts of water were forming 6-8' waves crashing over boulders. It was so loud we couldn't hear ourselves talk.

The rapids calmed down. Now, there were just boulders everywhere.

Was this the bay?

We couldn't see any river bank so we just turned North to find the cabin.

As I began to paddle, my hand dipped into the water and it became instantly <u>numb</u> — the water in Hudson Bay never gets over 32 degrees, even in the summer.

We had made it.

Oceans have waves, and this one was no exception. It also had boulders left by the glaciers. The trick to surviving was to keep the canoe from smashing into boulders while negotiating the waves.

Heading parallel to the shoreline put us broadside to the waves. This caused us to take in plenty of ice cold water necessitating a bailing-while-paddling technique. Stroke, Bail, Stroke, Bail — to capsize in water of this temperature would cause death by hypothermia within minutes.

"Where's the cabin?"

We finally passed the north shore of the Seal River with no sign of it.

"Does this thing exist or is it just more bullshit?"

We canoed on.

Spotting what looked like a bird standing on a unusual looking rock, we canoed by it.

"What's that?"

"Dead whale."

"OK, lets not hit it."

We canoed some more, still no cabin in sight.

"What if there is no cabin?"

We were so exhausted that we would be unable to continue much longer. We had already canoed about 30 miles that day and they weren't easy miles either.

We debated camping where we were at, but did not want to be in a tent because of the large white carnivores that frequent the area.

Also, the tide goes in and out about 12 miles and we didn't know if it was in or out. Maybe that was the problem. Maybe the tide is out and we are actually 12 miles offshore. That would not be a good situation!

What we hoped was the actual shoreline — *which we could see from the canoe* — was flat, strewn with boulders, and devoid of trees. The look is fairly consistent, so anything man-made would definitely stick out.

And eventually we did see something far in the distance that might be square. It didn't really look like a "cabin," but at least it didn't look like a boulder.

We headed towards it.

Having a goal renewed some of our depleted energy, and the closer we got, the better it looked.

Then — *at last* — we were there, and yes indeed, there was a cabin on Hudson Bay.

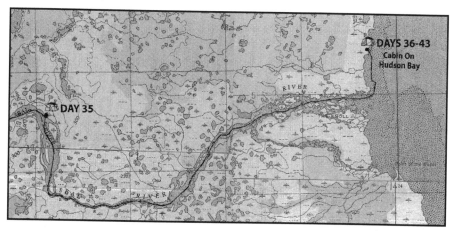

The Cabin on Hudson Bay

The cabin was about the size of a single wide mobile home and apparently was used as a goose hunting camp at certain times of the year.

Nearby, there was a small building with a generator in it.

We were hoping the door to the main cabin wasn't locked.

Approaching the door, we found only a latch, opened it, and walked in.

A large kitchen area greeted us.

It looked like a great place to hang out considering our past accommodations on this trip. The only problem was that all the windows were boarded up making it very dark.

It was light enough, however, to read the note written on the kitchen wall that stated...

"This place is hell without a gun."

That was comforting.

The next room contained several beds and a heater. Fred had made it to the back room and was yelling at me.

"Hey, check this out."

He had found a bullet hole in the wall with a note saying, "I was shooting at a bear in the room behind you."

Apparently the doors are unable to keep out a bear that wants to visit.

The prospect of polar bears breaking down the doors and chasing us around the cabin made us slightly uncomfortable, but after what we had already been through, it was just something else to deal with.

We checked around for escape routes and rigged up a rope so we could access the roof if we had to.

Then, totally exhausted, we crashed — on real beds!

Inside the cabin...
it was a cold day!

I awoke to a loud bang. The cabin shook.

I immediately thought the worst, but wasn't sure what was going on.

I faded back to sleep.

Bang! I woke up again.

Fred and I decided we had better investigate. We got up and cautiously looked around. No bears. Everything looked OK. Back to sleep.

Bang!

Light poured into the cabin — something had broken in, and the best guess was that it was a bear!

We jumped up, ready to make a run for it, only to see that one of the shutters on one of the windows had come loose and was flapping in the wind.

We had a good laugh, assured ourselves that the bears were further south at this time of year, and went back to sleep.

Day 37

According to our best calculations, it was Friday, July 17, 1981 and we had 4 days before we were to be picked up.

It seemed as if luck had turned our way, too, because in the kitchen was a large unopened jar of instant coffee! A major score.

Our entertainment now consisted of playing guitar, smoking reefer, drinking coffee, and thinking about how those steaks and beers would soon be a reality!

Our first day at the cabin we celebrated making it down the Seal River alive by smoking all the roaches we had saved from all the joints we smoked after all the rapids we ran.

We copped a superbuzz.

The Roach Joint

Of course, shortly thereafter, we heard a small boat motor and were soon visited by Eskimos.

They looked exactly like you'd expect Eskimos to look. Except for one thing — their parkas with the fur around the hood looked like it came from Wal Mart rather than being made from caribou or whale skins.

The Eskimos were, appropriately, on their way to Eskimo Point, a settlement to the North. They said they would never stay at the cabin we were in because it was <u>haunted</u>.

After telling us some very weird stories, they left.

Hudson Bay is a unique and interesting part of the planet and there are a number of theories on how it was formed. My favorite is the one about a giant meteor slamming into the earth. The shape fits.

The land around the bay — *at least where we were* — is perfectly flat, and being true tundra, there are no trees, not even scrubby little sticks.

Treeless Tundra

Most of the area is strewn with boulders and rocks of various sizes.

This is attributed to the glaciers which were so thick and heavy in this area, the land is still rising 8 millimeters per year.

Although the larger plants are missing, there is still a great variety of ground cover and flowers to explore especially if you are willing to do it on your hands and knees. Which, of course, we did... not much else to do.

Tundra Flowers

And now, the moment you've been waiting for,
and the thrilling conclusion to this story.

But first, a little background information...

The cabin we were in was located about 30 miles north of a town called Churchill in the Canadian Province of Manitoba.

The Churchill area is famous for its polar bears and they are a draw for tourists.

Now, our theory that "the bears are too far south to be a problem for us" was based on migratory research we did before we left on the trip.

According to the traditional patterns we learned about, the bears migrate South of Churchill during the summer and it's not until later in fall that they gather in the Churchill area, and the town itself, to wait for the ice to form on Hudson Bay so they can catch seals.

A Wall Street Journal article, however, that was given to me several years after our trip, has provided a "light bulb moment" on our experiences with the polar bears at the <u>cabin</u>.

When the bears gather in the town of Churchill, it may be good for tourism, but there can be problems and according to the WSJ article, *"incorrigible bears are trapped and held in "bear jail. When the bear facility fills up, the inmates are tranquilized and airlifted by helicopter to the **Seal River wilderness**, about 25 miles to the north."*

The article goes on to report one store owner's comment that, *"the best thing that could happen for tourism here is for **someone to be eaten every few years**."*

So, unknown to us at the time, it's likely that the worst problem polar bears were being relocated to the exact area where we were now staying, and of course, any problems we may have, like getting <u>eaten</u>, would be **good for business**.

And now, back to our story...

Day 38

It was day number two at the cabin.

Fred went off somewhere to take a shit.

I opened the cabin door, walked out, and started taking a piss.

As I surveyed the rugged arctic terrain I suddenly noticed there was a polar bear about 25 yards in front of me. It was <u>huge</u> — *the bears in this area weigh up to 1,500 pounds* — and it was <u>staring at me</u>.

I was concerned for Fred.

Was I going to be breakfast, or did it <u>already</u> eat my canoeing partner?

"Fred! Polar Bear!"

Slowly, I moved away from the bear towards the area where Fred was. The bear started walking away. As Fred returned — *intact* — the bear lumbered into the ocean and swam away.

My New Friend

So much for the "Bears Are Too Far South Theory."

From that point on, we had 2-3 bears hanging out with us at all times at a distance of 20 yards to 1/4 mile.

We would get stoned and watch them.

Polar Bear Facts

Description — Polar Bears are large white carnivorous furry things that weigh up to 1500 pounds. They feature 12" paws with very long, sharp, claws and 42 jagged teeth designed for tearing flesh.

Capabilities — A polar bear can outrun a race horse, swim 100 miles without stopping, smell lunch from 30 miles away, and leap tall icebergs in a single bound

Diet — Seals are preferred, but they will also eat whales, muskox, reindeer, rodents, birds, shellfish, fish, eggs, kelp, berries, and canoers.

Vacation — Polar bears like to eat warm juicy seals and most of their eating and hunting is done in the winter on the frozen ice of Hudson Bay. During this season, they fatten up so they can take the summer off and just wander up and down the coast. As summer goes on, however, they get hungrier and hungrier for a tasty seal. In early fall they begin to converge on Churchill, which has the highest concentration of Polar Bears in the world, to wait for the ice to freeze.

I made a few attempts to get some good pictures of the bears near the cabin, but the wide angle lens on my camera made them look like white dots that were hard to distinguish from the boulders that were strewn about the landscape.

And getting up close had its risks.

One day we were getting stoned while watching a polar bear that was sleeping in the grass about 30 yards away, so I decided to see if I could sneak up and get a shot. I quietly approached the sacked-out bear. Standing on a boulder I raised the camera just as the bear <u>woke</u> up and <u>stood</u> up.

Retreat!

I slowly walked backwards. It walked away. I <u>didn't</u> get the shot, but I didn't get <u>eaten</u> either.

We got used to having the bears around. They didn't appear to want to harm us. At night we could hear them outside the cabin knocking stuff over and we could feel them bump into the building, but they didn't break down the door.

During the day, we would watch them fight among themselves. It was some of the best entertainment we had during entire trip.

Our most <u>vulnerable</u> activity with regards to the bears, was collecting fresh water, presumably from the same place they get it — a small pond about 1/2 mile away from the cabin. With no trees or any other protection, if a bear wants you for lunch while you're out there, all you can do is pass it the salt.

The water expeditions, however, went without incident.

The Water Hole

View of the cabin from the water hole

Day 39

The next day was supposed to be our pick up day, so Fred decided to celebrate by cleaning up the kitchen. Some previous inhabitants had left a lot of garbage around, which attracts bears. So we dumped it all in a barrel and started to burn it.

Apparently polar bears love grilled garbage and must have thought we were having a party!

They started streaming in.

A Polar Bear Approaches

We climbed onto the roof.

View from the roof

We didn't know how long we would have to be on the roof and we didn't have any food or water. What if the bears just stayed close by and waited for us to come down?

They could take shifts — there were <u>three</u> of them and only <u>two</u> of us.

Anyway, they returned to a safe distance after a while, but we were concerned that they would now have a heightened interest in our presence.

Fred on Polar Bear watch

To celebrate our predicament I wrote a blues song...

The Polar Bear Blues

I was campin' in the Arctic where there ain't no trees,
Way up in the tundra with that crazy Arctic breeze,
I was sittin' in a cabin 50 miles out of town,
When up comes a Polar Bear and breaks the door down.

I got the polar bear blues (he's gonna eat me)
I got the polar bear blues (he's gonna chow down on me)
I got the polar bear blues ('cause he's got the munchies)
Throw me my running shoes!...

He said he'd been walkin' on the ice where he roamed,
Stopped by a friend's house and got pretty stoned,
He said how ya doin', my name is Steve,
And I got the munchies like you wouldn't believe!

I got the polar bear blues (he's gonna eat me)
I got the polar bear blues (he's gonna chow down on me)
I got the polar bear blues ('cause he's got the munchies)
Throw me my running shoes!...

I walked right up, but those claws looked pretty mean,
His teeth were sharp and I hoped this was a dream,
The bear licked his chops and assured me it was not,
He said I'm going to tear you up and cook you in a pot!

I got the polar bear blues (he's gonna eat me)
I got the polar bear blues (he's gonna chow down on me)
I got the polar bear blues ('cause he's got the munchies)
Throw me my running shoes!...

Fred was busy, too.

In anticipation of our return to civilization, and the prospect of returning our rented canoe — *which had picked up more that a few dents* — Fred attempted some repair work with a rock and a stick.

Fred tries to preserve some of our security deposit by pounding dents out of our rented canoe

Day 40

Today was the day! We packed up our stuff for the pick up.

The tide came in...

The tide is in

The tide went out...

The tide is out

No pick up.

Maybe the water was too rough or something.

While we were hoping someone would come the next day, the idea that no one was going to pick us up began to set in, and we discussed our alternatives.

If we canoed the bay, we would be taking a <u>very</u> serious risk. The main problem is that the tide comes in and goes out as much as 12 miles twice a day.

When the tide is in, there's water. When it's out, there is only mud and boulders for as far as one can see.

The rate at which it comes and goes is pretty amazing, too. One day I was washing dishes as the tide retreated and I started running after it, jumping from boulder to boulder, yelling, *"Hey, come back here, I'm not done yet!"*

But that didn't work, and I had to wait until the tide came back to finish the dishes.

Dirty dishes are a minor consequence of tidal movements.

Canoeing is a different matter. If you catch the tide, canoe out, and a storm blows up (Hudson Bay is noted for quick and violent storms), you're in big trouble because Swhen the tide starts coming back, you're 12 miles out in an ocean of 32 degree water with nowhere to go.

And it is the ocean with ocean waves — we barely it made to the cabin in fairly calm conditions.

And then there is the matter of tent camping with the Polar Bears along with all our food that can't be hung from a tree for safety because there aren't any.

Day 41

Today was the day! We packed up our stuff for the pick up.

The tide came in...

The tide went out...

No pick up.

Something was definitely <u>wrong</u>.

Fred and I discussed the situation. There <u>was</u> one other alternative to canoeing The Bay and that was to flag a plane.

We had observed that every now and then a DC3 would fly across the horizon towards the South bringing supplies to Churchill. If we could <u>signal</u> one of the planes they would probably contact the guy who was supposed to pick us up.

We decided to give it 3 days.

If we were not successful, then we would canoe the bay.

Fred on the shore with the tide out

Days 42-43

Two days went by constantly listening for planes and other signs of civilization with no luck.

On one of the days, we spotted a small boat and ran out yelling and shooting off firecrackers, but we failed to make an impression, and the boat moved on.

Moon over "The Bay of No Pickups"

Day 44

On the third day, we heard a plane in the distance.

We ran for our signal mirrors. The plane was about 10 miles to the south.

Even though we were convinced that the plane was so far away that the signal mirrors wouldn't work, we aimed them at the cockpit anyway. To our total amazement, the plane began to bank and head our way. As it flew overhead, we shot off a signal flare. We were saved. Someone knew we were here!

A couple hours went by. We heard the sound of a motor. The boat!

Didn't sound like a boat. It sounded like a helicopter.

It was a helicopter. Shit.

It landed and a Canadian Mountie got out with two .357 Magnum

Handguns strapped on his belt. We asked him about that, he mentioned that he <u>never</u> comes out this way without adequate <u>firepower</u> because of the polar bears.

"So, what's the problem?," he asked.

We explained our situation… our pick up didn't show up, we were surrounded by polar bears, and we didn't want to canoe Hudson Bay.

He mentioned that the helicopter costs $150 an hour.

We said, *"Well then, lets <u>go</u>."*

Landing strip with cabin in background

We were able to take all of our stuff except the canoe. The helicopter couldn't handle it. We would have to come back later and get it, or just leave it out there.

The chopper ride gave us an aerial view of the rapids we had canoed a few days previous.

They didn't look any <u>easier</u> from above.

We landed and paid for the ride.

Normally they don't have helicopters in the area, but National Geographic was doing a film called "Polar Bear Alert" and this was their research helicopter.

We did appreciate the fast service. If we were injured, it would have been important. They did the right thing, but we would have preferred a less dramatic exit from the area.

We now went looking for John Hicks, the guy who was <u>supposed</u> to handle our pick up, to see <u>what the fuck happened</u>.

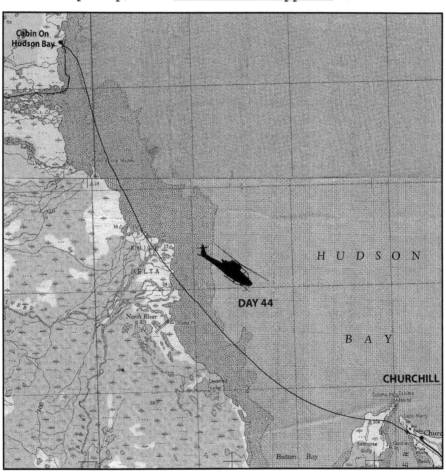

151

Churchill

John Hicks wasn't around, but we found his wife. It seems that they did get the message that we would be coming out early, but at the Caribou River, not the Seal.

They had gone looking for us twice and were just about to contact the Mounties to report us missing.

So now, in addition to the chopper charges, we owed the Hicks for 2 pickup attempts.

And we still didn't have our canoe.

The Hicks were accommodating, however. Since we were also staying at their hotel, we worked out a deal that didn't set us back too much, and the deal included retrieving the canoe.

To pick up the canoe, we needed a day when the weather was good at the same time the tide was in. Apparently that's not an easy combination to come by up there, so meanwhile, we were stuck in Churchill.

Churchill is a weird town. It was built to provide a shorter shipping route to Europe for Canadian grain exports. Unfortunately, it can only be reached 2 months out of the year and insurance on the freighters is almost prohibitively high because of icebergs.

So the town depends on tourism.

The local population consists of Drunkin' Indians on welfare and white people who own businesses.

The two groups do NOT get along.

The town bar has 2 sections — one for the white people and the other for Indians.

We mostly drank on the Indian side because it was a lot more fun. That was where we met Dave, a retired Indian trapper.

He was one of the funniest people I have ever met. We traded stories for hours.

Dave swore a lot... *"That fuckin' Caribou river you never would have made it, it's all fuckin' rapids. Fuckin' Caribou river. I've seen that fuckin' river. Never make it in no fuckin' canoe. Fuckin' Seal's not much fuckin' better. Fuckin' polar bears. Fuck Fuck Fuck Fuck."*

We visited him at his cabin, drank beers, and laughed a lot.

The only other thing to do in Churchill is to take tourist trips to see the polar bears, but we had seen enough of them.

We did spend a lot of time telling stories to the tourists and locals. Word travels fast in a small town, and we had achieved a degree of notoriety and respect for our exploits.

We heard some good stories about the area, too. Someone told us that the plastic we saw by the cabin on Hudson Bay was from an airplane. A polar bear had turned the plane upside down and beat on it all night with the pilot in it!

Other stories we heard about the bears made us realize that we lucked out with our buddies on Hudson Bay.

Churchill Shopping

The day finally came when conditions were good enough to get the canoe.

John Hicks hires a person to take care of the pickups on Hudson Bay and he was an interesting individual to hang out with for a day.

This person hates polar bears and told us he would shoot one as long as he didn't get caught (the polar bears are a protected species). In fact, he told us he would shoot anything he could.

In the winter, he traps out in the tundra for three months with the temperature as low as minus 90 — *yikes!*

The pay is good though. In those 3 months he can earn $10,000 (in "1981 dollars") and there aren't too many places to spend money in the tundra so it's almost all profit.

With the money he made the year before, he bought the boat we were taking to get our canoe.

The boat was actually a large wooden canoe with a motor. He was the one who had tried to pick us up at the Caribou River twice and it was his boat we had seen while we were at the cabin on the bay.

"You guys were at that cabin?"

"Yeah, we saw a boat and were shooting firecrackers the day you were out to pick us up."

"That was me, I stopped to shoot a seal. Too bad I didn't see you."

"Great"

Our of curiosity, we asked him how many people he's picked up at the Caribou River. He said, *"I've never picked anyone up at the Caribou River."*

> *In retrospect, I find it surprising that the Manitoba Government promoted canoeing down the Caribou River in their official "Manitoba Canoe Guide" (which is where we got the idea for this trip), when everyone we ran into — the people who know the area well — seemed to think that route was assured death by canoe.*

On the way to the cabin we went near a school of beluga whales that were jumping out of the water like dolphins. Beluga whales are pure white and about 20 feet long. At one point, they were nearly extinct having been vigorously hunted for many years. Now they are protected and seem to be rather plentiful.

We also buzzed a couple of polar bears in the water.

The bears <u>really</u> didn't like that and did everything they could to try get into our boats and eat us.

As I mentioned before, my camera had a wide angle lens on it. So to get the picture below, we had to get <u>very</u> close to a very annoyed bear. I still remember the snorting sound it made as I hung over the side of the boat to get the shot.

We arrived at the cabin just as the tide started to roll <u>out</u>.

Fred and I ran to the canoe and started dragging it to the boat. The boat guy was yelling at us to hurry or we'd be spending the night there. That gave us plenty of incentive to hurry.

As we left the cabin area, the boat was starting to bottom out as the water got lower and lower. We barely made it out.

On the way back to Churchill, we came across a couple of canoes that had just come out of another river. The boat guy approached them...

"Hey want a ride?"

"Sure"

"Throw me a rope."

They seemed real pleased to get towed back to Churchill until our guy made too sharp of a turn, flipped the canoes, and sent the occupants into the freezing water.

They were tied in with spray covers, so Fred and I prepared to go in after them, but they all popped up, <u>cold</u> but <u>safe</u>.

Their cameras and related gear, however, was destroyed.

Happy Canoers just before getting dumped into Husdon Bay

We had all our stuff, now we just needed a train to take us back to The Pas.

The train came.

We were told they had seats for <u>us</u>, but they said they couldn't take our <u>canoe</u> because the baggage car was full from some boy scout troop that had come down the Churchill River.

157

Fred gave the ticket lady a "take us or I'll kill you look."

They found room.

The train trip back to The Pas is a 24-hour ride. We were looking forward to just relaxing, reading some magazines, and having some drinks.

But the adventure wasn't over just yet...

While we were in Churchill we had heard that Sam the Indian had flown into town with the chief. As you may recall, Sam was the guy with the radio from Tadule Lake who had contacted John Hicks about our revised pickup plans.

We thought we had seen him in town a few times, but he appeared to be quite drunk and obnoxious. Fortunately, we were able to successfully duck the situation while we were in Churchill.

Now, on the train ride back The Pas — *glad to have escaped all the loonies in Churchill* — we went into the bar car for a drink, and guess who was there?

Good guess.

Sam was sober when we sat down, so all was well. We talked about our trip down the Seal River and our pick up problem on Hudson Bay. Sam insisted he had given John Hicks the right message and had even flown over us on the way to Churchill to see how we were doing.

I have no reason to doubt Sam's word. We'll never know how the message got garbled, nor does it matter.

We had a couple of drinks with Sam and his wife. As the drinks kicked in (2 beers), Sam began to transform from a nice down-to-earth person into a Drunken Indian and we decided it was best to get out of the bar before it got too ugly.

The Indians really can't handle alcohol very well and watching the transformation from Normal Indian to Drunken Indian is quite amazing. It's also very sad to see a person you came to like and respect in one environment become unbearable in another.

Back at our seats, we agreed that if we spotted Sam we would pretend we were <u>sleeping</u>.

It wasn't long before Sam walked into the car and we assumed the sleeping position. But it didn't work. Sam started shaking my arm.

"Hey lets go to dinner."

"OK"

I went to diner with Sam and his wife. Fred was smart and stayed at his seat.

At this point, Sam was really getting out of control and so was his wife. She kept telling me that Sam knew the cure for cancer but wouldn't tell anybody.

I asked him about it and he wouldn't tell me either.

The waiter soon cut Sam off from drinks for which I was grateful.

Sam then kept asking <u>me</u> to get more drinks for him.

"I took care of you guys. Come on, just one more."

I kept telling him we were <u>all</u> cut off.

Finally, I got away. Someone told me that when the Indians get too out of control they just stop the train and throw them off, even if it's in the middle of nowhere. That way, they can sober up and wait for the next train.

Sam got off — *or was thrown off* — somewhere half-way down the line.

We could finally rest in peace.

The last train stop was The Pas where we had begun our trip.

All we had to do was pick up the truck and turn in the canoe. We assumed we would lose our security deposit on the canoe because it was certainly <u>not</u> the canoe it used to be.

We went to the owner's shop. He said to drop the canoe off at his house and stop by the next morning.

Meanwhile, we went to get interviewed by the local newspaper. Once again, word of our exploits had traveled quickly.

The next day, the shop owner — *who either had not checked out his boat (unlikely) or felt partially responsible for almost getting us killed by renting us a boat like that (he <u>knew</u> where we were going!)* — gave us <u>all</u> of the security deposit back, plus a partial refund on the rental since we had not been gone as long as we had originally anticipated.

We took the cash, jumped in the truck and got out of town fast. Then we drove out West where we almost got killed mountain climbing.

But that's a whole 'nother story.

A special message from the publisher...

Thanks for your interest in *How to Canoe in Canada almost get killed by rapids, eaten by polar bears, have your blood sucked out by clouds of mosquitoes, and other fun stuff!*

I hope you enjoyed the journey!

I also hope that if you liked this book, you'll help us "spread the word" by letting others know about it.

We'd really appreciate it!

For all other comments and contacts you can send us a message via the contact form at *www.obepub.com*.

Other books from Old Barn Publishing

A History of World War Two Told in Letters, Stories of Romance, and Vintage Photos by Barbara Storm Farr

The Awakening of Surry County by Tom Scheve

For additional titles, book descriptions, purchase options, and to subscribe to receive updates, early notifications and special offers, visit obepub.com.

Do <u>you</u> have a story to tell?

Visit us at obepub.com to learn how you can get your stories into e-book and print formats. Today's technology makes it both practical and economical even if your audience is just family and friends (if it's larger, we may end sending you some nice royalty checks!). In any case, don't let your stories and experiences get lost. Books — *both electronic and printed* — are the perfect way to preserve information for future generations... and a fun and rewarding project for <u>you</u>, the author! ***Check out the possibilities at obepub.com.***

Printed in Great Britain
by Amazon